the salad project

the salad project

CLEM HAXBY

**How to build
unlimited salads**

Contents

008	Introduction
022	Crunches + Kicks
032	Creamy
072	Zingy
114	Herby
152	Spicy
195	Weekly Menus
202	Index
207	Thank Yous

Hello

from James + Florian, Co-Founders of The Salad Project.

Although we didn't know it yet, our enrolment at the École Hôtelière de Lausanne (EHL) in Switzerland was to be the start of both our friendship and our salad journey. Five years after graduating, having taken diverging paths into the hospitality industry and neither of us wholly satisfied, we launched The Salad Project in London's vibrant Spitalfields Market during the uncertain times of the COVID-19 pandemic.

Our mission was clear: to transform the fast-casual dining scene by focusing on superbly crafted salads served with five-star hospitality. The response from Londoners was nothing short of phenomenal. We've become a staple for those in the city seeking fresh, delicious and nutritious food, fast. Early in our journey, our commitment to quality and innovation was recognised when we were named Uber Eats Restaurant of the Year. That award, and the hefty queues that still stop us in our tracks on a daily basis, demonstrate an ever-growing demand for salad made better.

At the heart of our success is Clem, our Culinary Director. Under her guidance, The Salad Project has been, and continues to be, committed to setting new standards for what you should expect from a salad, from fresh flavours to generous portions.

There's no better feeling than seeing you in our restaurants every day – but we thought it was about time we started spreading our passion for salad made better into your own homes. So, we set about writing a cookbook that we hope inspires you to set new standards for your own salad design. A book filled with fresh, healthy food intended to fuel busy lives, providing you with formulas to explore your own creativity when it comes to salad.

We generally don't like to follow the status quo, so we've flipped traditional salad recipe books on their head. We believe big flavour comes from freshly made dressings – they're what define the character of our most popular salads in store. We've put dressings at the heart of this book, and from there, you can explore so many of our favourite salads, and discover your own.

We hope you enjoy digging into this book, and that you might pop in and see us in person if you haven't already. We're not sure how many sites we'll have when you read this, but you can guarantee we'll be working on getting one to your neighbourhood.

Cheers to fresh, delicious and nutritious food that's always fully dressed.

James + Florian

The Author

My name is Clem and I'm the Culinary Director at The Salad Project, which means I'm fortunate enough to design the food and manage the kitchens for the fastest-growing salad bar in London.

The Salad Project launched in 2021, but my own salad project started back in 2013 when salad represented the golden ticket for a teenage girl searching for some control during a chaotic phase of life. For so many years, salads have represented a meal that allows you to put as little into your body as possible. At 17, I was lured into its trap and lost control of any sense of food as something positive that you should want to put into your body in abundance.

Fortunately, my salad project changed course a few years later, when I completed a diploma in nutrition and qualified as a personal trainer. I wanted to flip the narrative of 'cutting out' instead of 'putting in' by educating myself in the benefits (and necessity) of positive food and fitness.

That chapter led me to enrol at Ireland's Ballymaloe Cookery School. At Ballymaloe, I fell in love with food. It reignited three passions that underpin the work I do at The Salad Project and, ultimately, in this book:

+ A passion for flavour, in all its delicious forms.
+ A passion for food as joyful, whether shared or indulged in alone.
+ A passion for food as fuel, and all the epic things it allows us to do when we eat well.

Now, my salad project is one defined by an utter obsession with deploying the most powerful tool we have at our disposal in life – food – to its fullest potential every single day. I bring this to everything I do at The Salad Project.

I'm on a mission to synonymise salad with abundance, energy and hefty portions of nothing but goodness. Through these recipes, I've employed the knowledge I've picked up along the way, and my understanding of what it means to be busy in life while striving for balance. Life is too short for boring food, and certainly too short to find yourself burned out from lack of effective fuelling, so it seems obvious to me that delicious, nutritious food should be faff-free and accessible to everyone living with busy schedules.

Whether you're in the first or fiftieth chapter of your salad project, I hope The Salad Project will help align us all in recognising the power of salad in its new, bigger and better era.

Clem

It All Starts with the Dressing

At The Salad Project, the final step in ordering a salad is choosing what to dress it with. Nine times out of ten, however, it is the dressing that pulls you towards a salad in the first place. As much as I wish we did, we simply don't crave chopped cucumber or baby spinach to the same extent that we crave the mouth-coating umami of a salty Caesar dressing, or the dribble-inducing acidity of a good apple cider vinaigrette. While it may be the last element we add to a salad (always at the last minute, please), a dressing has the power to turn an agglomeration of incohesive vegetables, proteins and crunches into a dish with real personality and purpose.

Despite this, dressings are too often sidelined in salad recipes. This book puts dressings where they belong: in the spotlight.

When I design a salad, I always think about the dressing first, to satiate our customers' cravings. I then select the ingredients that best pair with the dressing in question, considering the characteristics of those ingredients – texture, flavour, colour, weight – to arrive at a salad that is well balanced, bold and, of course, always fully dressed.

In this book, we bring you our favourite dressing recipes. Each dressing is paired with two salads alongside further suggestions for use, to show just how versatile these beautiful sauces can be for transforming simple ingredients into something delicious. We will give you multiple uses for your dressing in a week, allowing you to live by our principle of big flavour, fast.

Big Flavour, Fast

At The Salad Project, we focus on ensuring busy customers joining us on their precious lunch-breaks are able to pick up their salads as quickly as possible. The priority is nourishing people with simple, creative and curated food to fuel their busy lifestyles, without taking up their time.

Too often, dressings that go beyond a bit of honey, vinegar and crusty mustard from the back of your fridge can feel overwhelming to prep – let alone shop for – after a long day. Did we finish that bottle of soy sauce? Is that jar of harissa still kicking about in the fridge?

This book encourages you to take the stress out of the day to day, leaving only the simple decisions for your midweek supermarket drop-in. Following our best practice will ensure that, regardless of those delirious decisions, you have what you need in the fridge to make a dinner that is always fully dressed and flavourful.

Quality Nutrients, Colour + Concentrated Flavours

As you should hopefully recognise by now, I believe dressings are pretty powerful.

Everybody loves the spicy green citrus of Mexican cooking, or the comforting combination of peanut and chilli that emanates throughout Thai cuisine. But it's not always that simple to bring those flavours into your cooking repertoire if you're short on time or energy. Salad dressings allow you to capture and concentrate those flavours in one recipe that takes five minutes to prep at the start of your week. You can then pull them out of the fridge at any moment, turning neutral ingredients into something loaded with character.

But dressings go further than just providing punchy flavours. They can also serve as nutritional boosts to the meals they dress.

At The Salad Project, we don't believe in restricting what you eat. Instead, we believe in fuelling our bodies with as many good things as possible. We build as many layers of these good things into our salads as we can – and our dressings are a key contributor.

Historically, the purpose of salads has been to deliver as few calories as possible, while serving up a (hopefully) satisfying meal. We take a different view: the value of a salad actually lies in just how many different nutrients you can bring into one dish. Whether you subscribe to sourcing your '5-a-day', or to packing in 30 plants per week, multi-layered salads are your most effective route to success.

This book does not aim to prescribe a specific diet, but rather a lifestyle that celebrates fuelling your body with quality nutrients, colour and creative flavours, all concentrated into simple prep methods that will fit in with even the busiest of schedules. But, because we know you're probably interested, we've highlighted recipes that are particularly hard-hitters when it comes to protein, brain fuel or gut happiness, so you can focus on a specific category if you feel inclined.

Our Dressing Formula

Balance is key when it comes to designing a dressing. I have constructed a formula intended to guide you through making your own, either from the get-go, or after you have explored and experimented with the dressings in this book.

Just as bestselling food writer and chef Samin Nosrat sees the mastery of cooking in the control of four key elements – salt, fat, acid and heat – I believe the mastery of dressings lies in the control of salt, acid, fat and sweet. Although some dressing recipes sway from these exact proportions, this is a reliable template with which to start:

SALT 5% + **ACID 30%** + **FAT 55%** + **SWEET 10%**

Our Salad Formula

Just as we have a formula for dressings, we also have a formula for curating our salads at The Salad Project. As a rule of thumb for building your own salads, here is how we recommend layering different ingredients:

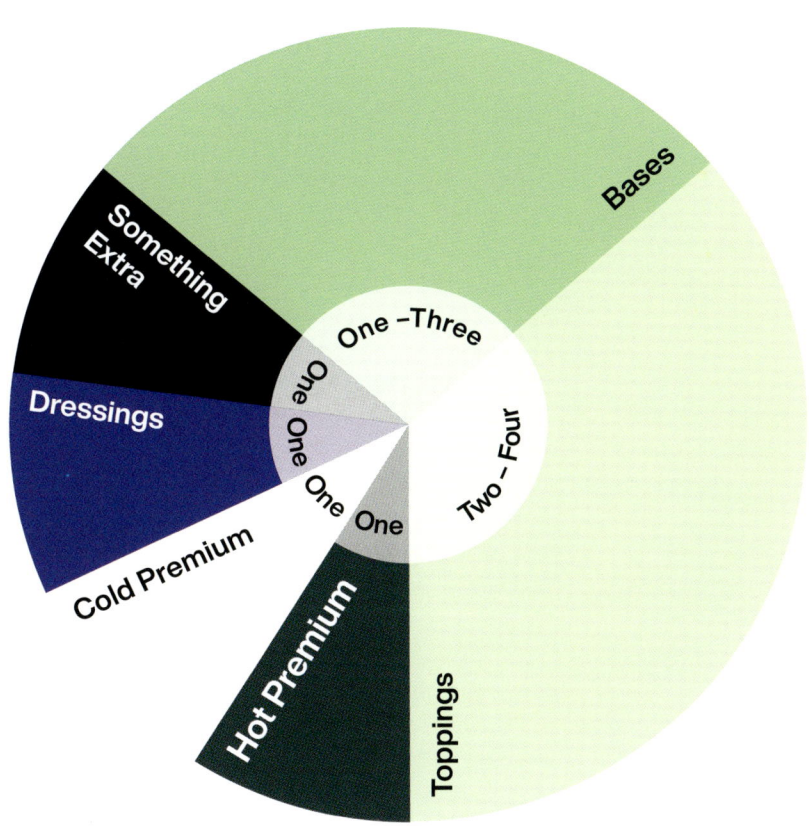

- **Leaves, grains, carbohydrates**
- **Small vegetables (cooked or raw) + crunches**
- **Protein or big-ticket vegetables**
- **Cold, big-ticket items like cheeses, dips or avocado**
- **The drizzle that will define your salad's character**
- **Citrus squeezes + sprinkles**

Here are the key ingredients that fall into each category of the dressing formula. Consider this a guide from which you can pull ideas and combinations, rather than an overwhelmingly long shopping list.

Salt

The word 'salad' derives from the Latin word for 'salted', so salad should, in short, never go without salt. When added to vegetables, salt encourages the release of water, enhancing their crispness and flavour. It also delivers an irresistible crunch in itself when sea salt flakes are sprinkled amid greens.

Sea salt – Available in both coarse and fine versions, sea salt is made from evaporated sea water. It is a very clean-tasting salt and can contain up to 60 trace minerals that offer healthy micronutrients.

Cooking salt – Saltier-tasting than sea salt, but less salty than table salt, this can also be known as 'kosher salt'. We'd recommend filling a salt caddy next to your hob, as it comes in handy for seasoning cooked dishes or cooking pastas and grains.

Soy sauce – Originating from China, soy sauce comes in a range of styles, including dark, light and sweet, all of which can bring a very individual character to dressing recipes. You can't go wrong by experimenting with whichever type you see on the shelf.

Tamari – A Japanese version of soy sauce, tamari is a by-product of miso production. Generally low in or free from gluten, it is less salty and more umami than soy sauce, with less variation in style and flavour.

White miso paste – This is made from soybeans fermented with a large proportion of rice. It is lighter and sweeter in flavour than red miso, so is our favourite miso for use in dressings.

Tinned anchovies – Filleted and salt-cured, tinned anchovies pack a salty, umami punch, both in creamy dressings and herby ones. They are also excellent dropped directly into a salad, so are always handy to have on hand.

Capers – The buds of the caper bush, these magical bites sit between olives and pickles in terms of flavour. Either way, they pack a salty punch thanks to their brine – which can also be used to add flavour to a dressing.

Preserved lemons – Originating from North Africa, these are whole, halved or quartered lemons packed into a salty brine. The preserving liquid means they lose their acidic, citrusy kick over time and instead take on a saline, fresh and umami flavour. You can eat the skin and flesh, and use the brine in dressings (or a vodka martini).

Parmesan – A hard cheese made from cow's milk in Northern Italy (in the provinces of Parma and Reggio Emilia), Parmesan is aged for a minimum of 12 months, which gives it a deep, umami flavour. Calf rennet is used to turn the milk into cheese, meaning it is not suitable for vegetarians. Vegetarian alternatives include some 'Italian hard cheese' and certain pecorinos.

Feta – A brined sheep's milk cheese originating from Greece. It is generally lower in calories than aged cheeses like Parmesan, but high in salt. It can be whipped into dressings to provide both salt and a creamy fat base.

Fat

Fat often acts as the base component of a dressing, suspending the salt, acid and sweet elements. However, fats also contribute a lot of character to a dressing, from adding creamy textures to earthy, nutty flavours.

Mayonnaise – Full-fat is your only option, every time, for the best flavour and texture.

Natural yoghurt – Again, opt for full-fat for the thickest texture, and to avoid added sugars that are used to replace some of the flavour and texture lost in lower-fat versions.

Crème fraîche or sour cream – Both are made from cultured milk. Crème fraîche is thicker and fattier, while sour cream is a little thinner and tangier.

Full-fat coconut milk or coconut yoghurt – Both are great options for substituting with animal-based products. When using canned coconut milk, start with the coconut cream before adding the separated water bit by bit, to avoid your dressing thinning out too much.

Tahini – A paste made from sesame seeds. Make sure to give your jar a good shake and stir each time you use it, to avoid ending up with a thick clump of paste that will change the consistency of your dressing.

Peanut butter – Smooth is best for use in dressings. Opting for deep roast can add an unrivalled depth of flavour if you are a peanut butter fan.

Cashew butter – See my notes on peanut butter!

Extra virgin olive oil – The least processed, highest-quality and richest-tasting olive oil you can buy. Extra virgin olive oil is loaded with polyphenols, which offer antioxidant and anti-inflammatory properties. It can be strong in flavour, so isn't suitable for all dressings.

Neutral olive oil – Generally labelled 'olive oil', this can be made from a blend of virgin and refined olive oils and has a lighter, more neutral taste, so it can be used for a greater variety of dressings.

Toasted sesame oil – This has a richer, nuttier flavour than regular sesame oil, and brings a delicious warmth to dressings.

Avocado oil – Loaded with oleic acid, polyunsaturated fats, carotenoids and other antioxidants, avocado oil is linked to improved heart, eye and skin health.

Acid

Acid plays a key role in adding zing and freshness to a dressing. Without it, a dressing can be flabby and lacking in character, getting lost in the mix of ingredients it is intended to elevate. Just as importantly, acid is vital to the texture of a dressing, as it emulsifies with the fat to create a smooth, creamy and well-distributed dressing.

White wine vinegar – Less acidic than apple cider vinegar, white wine vinegar is made from fermented white wine and can be mild and slightly sweet.

Red wine vinegar – Dark in colour, this offers a less acidic taste to its white wine counterpart.

Apple cider vinegar – Tart and sweet, apple cider vinegar retains a subtle fruitiness from the apples it is pressed from. It offers gut-health properties thanks to the bacteria and yeast cultures present in its production.

Balsamic vinegar – Produced by ageing pressed grapes in oak barrels, balsamic vinegar has a distinct sweet and zesty flavour. It can be complex and sweet, with the aged examples taking on increased viscosity and a higher price tag! Avoid 'balsamic glaze', which is made with the addition of sugars.

Rice wine vinegar – Used extensively in Asian cuisine, rice wine vinegar is produced from fermented rice. It has a sweeter flavour than red and white wine vinegars, but is still acidic and slightly salty. Don't confuse this with mirin – you can substitute the two, but the flavour profile will change considerably.

Lemon – Use for a bitter-sweet citrus flavour. One lemon generally gives you around 3–4 tablespoons, or 45–60ml, of juice.

Lime – More acidic and tart than lemons, you should get around 2 tablespoons, or 30ml, of juice per lime.

Sweet

If added in the right measures, sweetness should be barely detectable in a good salad dressing. We add sugar to round out dressings that would otherwise be overwhelmingly salty or acidic.

Caster sugar – Use for a simple sweetness that doesn't impart specific flavour, and dissolves evenly and easily into a dressing.

Soft light/dark brown sugar – Bringing a deeper, more caramel sweetness with marginally more minerals than white sugar, soft brown sugar dissolves very well into dressings and sauces.

Honey – A thick, floral syrup or paste that is 25 per cent sweeter than white sugar, meaning you can use a little less honey than you would sugar.

Agave – A syrup derived from the agave plant, agave is more neutral in flavour than honey and has a thinner consistency. It is suitable for plant-based diets, and is 150 per cent sweeter than white sugar, meaning you can use a lot less to achieve the same effect.

Maple syrup – A natural, golden sweetener made from the sap of maple trees, maple syrup is plant-based and produced according to specific quality criteria. It adds vanilla-y, butterscotch flavours to a recipe.

Pomegranate molasses – Made from reduced pomegranate juice, this has a sweet-sour tangy flavour and is most traditionally used in Middle Eastern recipes.

Date molasses – Made from reduced date juice, this is a sticky, sweet syrup that adds a deep bittersweet caramel flavour to recipes.

Mirin – A Japanese rice wine that adds a subtle, aromatic sweetness to dressings, mirin is particularly good as a sweetener.

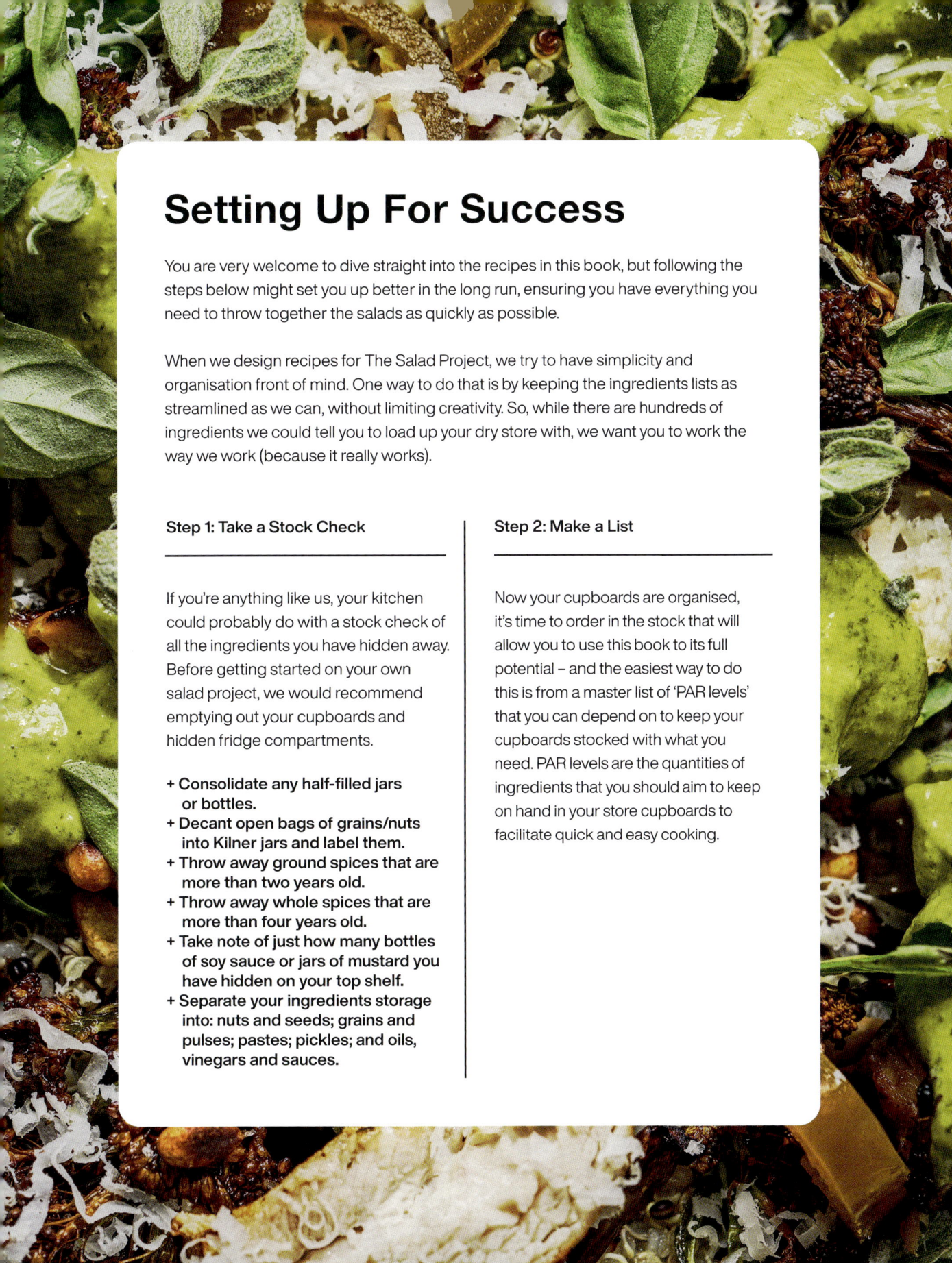

Setting Up For Success

You are very welcome to dive straight into the recipes in this book, but following the steps below might set you up better in the long run, ensuring you have everything you need to throw together the salads as quickly as possible.

When we design recipes for The Salad Project, we try to have simplicity and organisation front of mind. One way to do that is by keeping the ingredients lists as streamlined as we can, without limiting creativity. So, while there are hundreds of ingredients we could tell you to load up your dry store with, we want you to work the way we work (because it really works).

Step 1: Take a Stock Check

If you're anything like us, your kitchen could probably do with a stock check of all the ingredients you have hidden away. Before getting started on your own salad project, we would recommend emptying out your cupboards and hidden fridge compartments.

+ Consolidate any half-filled jars or bottles.
+ Decant open bags of grains/nuts into Kilner jars and label them.
+ Throw away ground spices that are more than two years old.
+ Throw away whole spices that are more than four years old.
+ Take note of just how many bottles of soy sauce or jars of mustard you have hidden on your top shelf.
+ Separate your ingredients storage into: nuts and seeds; grains and pulses; pastes; pickles; and oils, vinegars and sauces.

Step 2: Make a List

Now your cupboards are organised, it's time to order in the stock that will allow you to use this book to its full potential – and the easiest way to do this is from a master list of 'PAR levels' that you can depend on to keep your cupboards stocked with what you need. PAR levels are the quantities of ingredients that you should aim to keep on hand in your store cupboards to facilitate quick and easy cooking.

Your Kitchen PAR Levels

Kitchens come in all different shapes and sizes, so use this as a reference for when you're picking up ingredients, but don't fret about stocking up with everything at once if it means keeping miso in your underwear drawer. I've highlighted the non-negotiables in bold to get you started.

Salts

Sea salt – 1 pack of sea salt flakes
Cooking salt – 1 pack of fine cooking salt
Soy sauce/tamari – 1 litre (to avoid running out too quickly)
White miso paste – 1 large jar
Tinned anchovies – 2 tins
Capers – 1 large jar
Preserved lemons – 1 large jar
Parmesan – 250g
Feta – 200g

Fats

Full-fat mayonnaise – 1 large squeezy bottle
Natural yoghurt (or a plant-based equivalent) – 500g
Crème fraîche or sour cream – 400ml
Full-fat coconut milk – 400ml
Tahini – 450g jar
Sesame seeds – 100g
Peanut butter – 300g jar, preferably deep roast
Cashew butter – 170g jar
Extra virgin olive oil – 1 litre
Toasted sesame oil – 500ml
Avocado oil – 500ml

Acids

Red wine vinegar – 500ml
White wine vinegar – 500ml
Apple cider vinegar – 500ml
Balsamic vinegar – 500ml
Rice wine vinegar – 300ml
Lemons – 3
Limes – 3

Sweets

Caster sugar – 500g
Soft light brown sugar – 500g
Honey or agave – 1 bottle or jar
Maple syrup – 1 bottle
Pomegranate molasses – 1 bottle
Date molasses – 1 bottle
Mirin – 1 bottle

Spices

Smoked paprika – 1 jar
Cayenne pepper – 1 jar
Chipotle chilli flakes – 1 jar
Chilli flakes – 1 jar
Cumin seeds – 1 jar
Fennel seeds – 1 jar
Coriander seeds – 1 jar
Ground coriander – 1 jar
Ground cumin – 1 jar
Black pepper – whole peppercorns, in a grinder

Herbs

Flat leaf parsley – 25g
Coriander – 25g
Mint – 25g
Dill – 25g
Basil – 25g (this herb prefers room temperature storage and sunlight!)
Chives – 25g

Your Order of Work + Guide to Using this Book

Now you've done your stock check, ordered to your PAR levels and set up your kitchen, here is your order of work to help you embrace The Salad Project lifestyle:

Monthly Batch Prep

1. Take 45 minutes or so to stock up on 'Crunches + Kicks' (see Chapter 1) that will keep for weeks.

Weekly Batch Prep

1. Choose two or three dressings from this book.
2. Make a list of the ingredients you need to make them.
3. Compare this list with your dry and fresh stores.
4. Stock up on any ingredients that are missing.
5. Prep your chosen dressings (5 minutes), pour into jam jars, label and store in the fridge.

Service Time

1. Choose a salad recipe that pairs with one of your prepped dressings.
2. Organise a food delivery, or pick up the fresh ingredients on your way home.
3. Follow the recipe in under 30 minutes.
4. Finish with your ready-to-rock dressing and Crunches + Kicks (see Chapter 1).
5. Dress up your leftovers with the same dressing, or another from the fridge.

NOTE

+ Each dressing has two suggested recipe pairings – but they can also be used to mix-and-match with any salads in the same chapter, and to jazz up any leftovers or non-salad meals you might be making.
+ The dressings generally keep for up to 1 week in the fridge.

Your Week, Fully Dressed

Here is an example of what that would look like in a week.
To find more meal plan ideas, head to pages 195–199.

Vegetarian Salad Project

	Sunday	Monday	Tuesday
Prep or In Stock	The SP Green Goddess Dressing (see page 118) Sesa-Miso Dressing (see page 52) Toasted Furikake Seeds (see page 25) Maple Walnuts (see page 24) Quick Pickled Onions (see page 28)		
Salad		The plant-based GOAT (see tip on page 120)	Sesame Soy Tofu with Furikake Croutons + Pickled Chillies (see tip on page 54)

Wednesday	Thursday	Friday	Saturday
			Fresh Mint Drizzle (see page 140)
Clem's Potato Salad (see page 122)		Chilled Sesame Noodles with Balsamic Mushrooms, Lime Slaw + Toasted Furikake Seeds (see page 57)	Peaches + Cream (see page 144)

Selecting Your Recipes

We know food is personal, and there are a number of factors that will steer you towards certain recipes. We've used the following categories to help you identify the recipes that will work for you.

All our recipes let you know how long they should take and include icons to highlight what dietary requirements they suit. In many cases, we've suggested plant-based substitutions directly in the ingredients list, or via little 'tips' next to the recipe, to ensure vegetarians and vegans can make the most of as many salads in the book as possible.

Some of the recipes that we think are particular nutritional powerhouses have an additional label, outlined on the right. Look out for these dotted through the book.

Dietary Icons

- **(V) Suitable for vegetarian diets**
- **(VG) Suitable for vegan diets**
- **(GF) Suitable for gluten-free diets**
- **(PE) Suitable for pescatarian diets**

Intensity of Prep

+ **Quick-Build:** less than 20 minutes
+ **Medium-Build:** less than 30 minutes
+ **Long-Build:** more than 30 minutes

Nutrition Tags

+ **Protein Power:** Salads that focus on delivering complete animal or plant proteins for optimum recovery, muscle growth and energy.

+ **Brain + Body Fuel**: Salads that are built around the foods that best fuel our brains, and keep our blood sugar levels steady with slow-release carbohydrates.

+ **Gut Happy:** Salads that serve up the bits our guts love the best – including probiotic-filled ferments and high-fibre foods like whole grains, beans and leafy greens.

Crunches + Kicks 22–31

Excellent salads depend on elements that grab your attention in every bite: ingredients that cut through the noise with texture or a tongue-tingling touch of warmth. We've compiled a handful of our most powerful and effective kicks and crunches that feature time and time again in our recipes. Prep these in batches and they'll keep for ages in your cupboard or fridge, ready for deployment whenever your salad project may call for them.

Maple Walnuts

Serves 2

+ Medium-Build

220g walnuts
80g maple syrup
70g soft dark brown sugar
2 pinches of sea salt

The secret's out. These aren't very good for you … but if they'll get you eating salad, we think that's a healthy balance.

1. Preheat the oven to 200°C/180°C fan and line a medium-sized baking tray with parchment paper.
2. Weigh your walnuts into a bowl, then add the maple syrup, sugar and salt. Mix well, ensuring the sugar is dissolved and the walnuts fully coated. Pour onto the lined tray and use a rubber spatula to scrape all the maple syrup and sugar onto the walnuts.
3. Place in the oven for 10 minutes, then stir with a wooden spoon. (Note: the mixture will bubble in the heat, so don't panic if it looks very liquid when you take it out of the oven each time. Just give it a stir to coat the nuts.) Return to the oven for 10 minutes, then stir again.
4. Repeat for a final 10 minutes, stir and leave to cool on the tray.
5. Once cool, remove from the parchment paper and use your hands or a rolling pin to break up the walnuts. You can keep them whole, or crush them a little, before pouring them into a large glass jar and storing somewhere cool and dry for up to 3 weeks.

Crispy Onions

Serves 2

+ Quick-Build

2 white onions or 4 shallots
2 tsp cornflour
350ml vegetable oil
Fine cooking salt

Crispy onions are a real flavour bomb, adding both crunch and a salty, mellow onion taste. They are available to buy in the supermarket if you'd rather not fry your own – just be sure to read the label, as some contain gluten, which you may not want. Making them fresh really does add a pop of serious flavour, but the shop-bought ones will hold their crunch for weeks versus days.

1. Finely slice the onions or shallots using a knife or a mandolin – you can either slice into full rings or half moons. Place into a bowl. Add the cornflour and toss with your hands to lightly coat the onions.
2. Heat the oil in a saucepan over a medium heat – test it's reached a high enough temperature by dropping in a piece of onion and seeing if it sizzles. When it's hot enough, add the onions to the oil, working in batches to avoid overcrowding, and allow to fry until golden and crispy. Remove using a slotted spoon to a plate lined with kitchen paper. Season generously with salt and allow to cool while you cook the next batch.
3. Store in an airtight container for up to 4 days. If they go a little soft, just crisp them up in the oven for a couple of minutes.

Toasted Furikake Seeds

Serves 2

+ Quick-Build

A cracking store-cupboard friend to have. Toasted seeds, but that little bit more interesting. You'll find yourself reaching for these as a quick snack, and as seeds are an amazing source of omega-6 fats, among numerous other vitamins and minerals, we think of them as a nutrient shot that can be added to any dish to power it up. If you're plant-based, adding these seeds to your salads is the perfect way to turn incomplete plant proteins, like beans, pulses and whole grains, into complete ones, providing your body with the best of what it needs to recover and repair.

| 100g pumpkin seeds |
| 100g sunflower seeds |
| 1 tbsp furikake seasoning |
| 1 tbsp extra virgin olive oil |
| 1 tbsp sea salt |
| Grind of black pepper |

1. Preheat the oven to 200°C/180°C fan and line a baking tray with parchment paper.
2. Weigh your ingredients into a mixing bowl and mix until the seeds are fully coated and the ingredients are evenly distributed. Pour the mixture onto the lined tray and bake for 4 minutes. Stir and return to the oven for a further 4 minutes. Check the seeds – if the skins of the pumpkin seeds are splitting and the sunflower seeds are turning golden, they are ready to go. If not, return to the oven for a further 2 minutes until toasted.
3. Allow to cool, then pour into a glass jar and store somewhere cool and dry for up to 3 weeks (or until you run out!).

Sweet + Smoky Paprika Almonds

Serves 2

+ Quick-Build

A delicious way of adding some extra crunch, colour and plant power to any salad. You'll find out why these are a topping we keep coming back to in our salads. It's so easy to whip up a batch and keep them in your cupboard for later.

| 380g whole, skin-on almonds |
| 1½ tbsp smoked paprika |
| 1 tbsp soft dark brown sugar |
| ¼ tsp fine cooking salt |
| Pinch of sea salt |
| 2 tbsp extra virgin olive oil |

1. Preheat the oven to 200°C/180°C fan and line a baking tray with parchment paper.
2. Place all the ingredients into a mixing bowl and mix until the almonds are well coated. Pour onto the lined tray. Bake for 4 minutes, then stir and return to the oven for a further 4 minutes. Stir and return for 2 final minutes.
3. Allow to cool before pouring the almonds into a glass jar. Store somewhere cool and dry for up to 3 weeks.

Quick Pickled Onions

Serves 2

+ Quick-Build

1 red onion
1 tsp fine cooking salt
2 tsp caster sugar
150ml white wine vinegar
240ml boiling water

While slow ferments have so many incredible health benefits, and an incomparable complexity of flavour, you'll thank us for taking you down a slightly simpler route. Shake these up in minutes every couple of weeks – few dishes are worse off with pickled onions. Fact.

1. Cut the onion in half through the root and peel off the papery skin. Place cut side down on a chopping board with the root facing towards the hand you're keeping it steady with. Slice the onion as thinly as your knife skills allow, or use a mandolin to slice your onion into whole circle or half-moon slices, then repeat with the other half. Push down into a jar or airtight container.
2. Add the salt, sugar and vinegar, and stir well. Finally, add the boiling water and use a spoon to push the onion slices under the surface of the liquid. Put the lid on and give your jar or container a good shake to help dissolve the sugar and salt. Label and keep in your fridge for up to 2 weeks. Note: the onions will turn a bright pink within an hour or so – after a week, the colour will fade to a purple, but they are still fine to eat.

Pickled Chillies

Serves 2

+ Quick-Build

150g mixed chillies
2 tsp caster sugar
1 tsp fine cooking salt
100ml white wine vinegar

We prefer using pickled chillies over fresh chillies because, whenever we buy chillies, we use one and the rest are left to go mouldy in the corner of the vegetable drawer. By batch pickling, you can reduce that waste, but also reap the benefits of slightly mellowed spice levels and the probiotics that arise from the pickling process.

1. Slice your chillies into 2mm rings using a knife or a mandolin. Place the chilli slices and their seeds into a jar or airtight container.
2. Add the sugar, salt and vinegar and stir well. Finally, add boiling water until the chillies are just covered. Put the lid on and shake well to dissolve the sugar and salt, then label and leave to pickle for a minimum of 30 minutes. The longer you leave these, the more they will mellow and build tang. Keep in the pickled liquid in the fridge for up to 3 weeks.

Hot Honey

Serves 2

+ Quick-Build

150g runny honey
1 tsp cayenne pepper
1½ tsp chilli flakes
1 tbsp apple cider vinegar
1 tsp sea salt

Whether you drizzle this over your salads for a finishing salty-sweetness, or pour it onto your pizza, we won't know – but either way, it's a delicious store-cupboard staple that you can lean on when you're in need of a little zhuzh.

1. Measure the ingredients straight into a glass jar and use a spoon to mix well, then put the lid on. Store in a cool, dry place and stir before use – the spice will integrate more with time, so this is best used after it has had a couple of hours to sit. It will keep for up to 3 weeks.

Crispy Chilli Oil

Serves 2

+ Long-Build

250ml vegetable oil
3 shallots
½ tsp fine cooking salt
10 garlic cloves
150g roasted and salted peanuts
3 tbsp sesame seeds
1 tbsp soft dark brown sugar
2 tbsp tamari or light soy sauce
Pinch of sea salt
4 tbsp chilli flakes
2 tsp coriander seeds
1 cinnamon stick
2 star anise
8g ginger, peeled and finely chopped
1 tbsp Sichuan peppercorns

There are some great crispy chilli oils on the market, so you can pick up a jar and use that for recipes in this book. However, some are healthier than others, and we like to know exactly what goes into our food, so that's why we've created our own recipe for crispy chilli oil that takes 20 minutes to make. We've used coriander seeds for a citrusy, floral flavour – feel free to skip them, or switch in some fennel or cumin seeds if you prefer!

1. Heat the oil in a medium saucepan over a medium–high heat. While it's heating, halve the shallots through the root and peel off the skin. Using a mandolin or a knife, finely slice the shallots and add the small slices to the hot oil, along with the cooking salt. Fry for 8 minutes.
2. Meanwhile, peel the garlic and finely slice. After 8 minutes, add the garlic and peanuts to the pan and fry everything together until golden and crisp – depending on the size of your slices, this will take roughly another 7–10 minutes. Just be careful, as the garlic can burn suddenly, so keep an eye on it by stirring regularly.
3. While the shallots and garlic are frying, measure the sesame seeds, sugar, tamari or soy sauce, sea salt, chilli and coriander seeds into a heat-proof bowl.
4. Once the garlic and shallots are crispy and golden, place a sieve over a second heat-proof bowl and pour the oil through the sieve. Keep the oil and allow the garlic and shallots to sit in the sieve.
5. Pour the oil back into the saucepan and add the cinnamon stick, star anise, ginger and Sichuan peppercorns. Simmer over a medium heat to infuse the oil with the spices for 5 minutes. Pour the infused oil, along with the spices, over the sesame seed and chilli mix and stir. Add the fried onions, shallots and peanuts, and stir again.
6. Allow to cool fully before pouring into a glass jar. Keep in the fridge or in a cool, dark place for up to 3 weeks.

Creamy
32–71

A creamy dressing isn't the first thing that comes to mind when we think about whipping up a quick and easy salad at home. It's much easier, after all, to whack some vinegar, mustard, sugar and olive oil in a jar and give it a shake. But our experience at The Salad Project has taught us that the love for creamy dressings is very much alive and kicking – as is the curiosity to find new, creative combinations to keep them fresh.

So, this selection of recipes aims to show you just how simple it can be to create creamy dressings that pack a serious flavour punch in your own kitchen. It also hopes to demonstrate that there is so much more to 'creamy dressings' than a Caesar – although, of course, that makes an appearance.

We play with coconut milk, almond milk, natural yoghurt and tahini to show you creamy dressings don't always mean salad cream or mayonnaise. There are so many ways to reach that silky texture we all crave.

By using our tried-and-tested recipes, or curating your own with the guide opposite, you can ensure everything from crisp and crunchy lettuces to carbohydrates that can carry a little more weight will always be fully dressed.

KEY CHARACTERISTIC:

Silky smooth and simpler than you think

BEST WHEN:

Ice cold and combined with a crunch

BUILD YOUR OWN

Curate your own creamy combinations with this simple formula:

SALT   ACID   FAT   SWEET

The key element that shapes a creamy dressing is the fat.

FATS TO EXPERIMENT WITH:

+ Full-fat mayonnaise
+ Natural yoghurt (or plant-based alternatives)
+ Crème fraîche or sour cream
+ Full-fat coconut milk
+ Tahini
+ Sesame seeds
+ Peanut butter
+ Cashew butter

Balancing sweetness is less important for creamy dressings, so we focus more on what salts and acids can cut through the creamy base to create a dressing that's luscious in texture, but still bright and refreshing when tossed through a salad.

DOS AND DON'TS FOR CREAMY DRESSINGS:

+ Creamy dressings are, by their nature, heavier than vinaigrettes – avoid pairing them with delicate salad leaves that will wilt under their weight and give you a soggy, sad salad.
+ Creamy dressings can be thick or thin – keep it thick if you want a punchy dip, or a partner for potatoes or protein; thin it out with water or lemon juice if you want a looser coating for kale or noodles.
+ Creamy dressings don't mean dairy – swap out natural yoghurt for non-dairy yoghurts or sour cream for a plant-based mayonnaise.
+ Creamy dressings can thicken up in the fridge – just leave them at room temperature or give them a whisk to return them to your ideal consistency.
+ Creamy dressings don't need to go on top – dollop them as bases for platters, spread them underneath a plate of roasted vegetables or mix them completely into a potato salad.
+ Creamy dressings are best served cold – so keep it cool for a crisp contrast to your hot headliners.

CREAMY

Chipotle Caesar Dressing

Dresses 4–6 salads

As much as I hate to admit it, because it's more fun to develop fresh flavour combinations than follow the guidelines of old classics, this is a firm favourite among Salad Project devotees – our second-most popular dressing, in fact. It's my duty to protect its quality and consistency, so in the early days of The Salad Project, I made an oath never to sway away from Hellman's mayonnaise. I'd recommend you don't, either.

1. Grate your Parmesan using a microplane or a fine grater and set aside.
2. Peel and crush your garlic using the side of a knife or a garlic crusher and a little sea salt to help turn it into a smooth paste.
3. Place all the ingredients, excluding the water, into a blender and blitz until silky smooth. Gradually add the water and mix with a fork or small whisk until you reach your desired consistency. Play with the spice level by adding more cayenne pepper for a hotter Caesar, or more paprika for something a little smokier. Store in an airtight jar or container in the fridge for up to 1 week.

Ingredients
35g Parmesan
1 garlic clove
130g mayonnaise
1 tbsp Worcestershire sauce
1 tsp white wine vinegar
½ lemon (juice)
3 black peppercorns
Generous pinch of cayenne pepper, plus extra to taste (optional)
¼ tsp smoked paprika, plus extra to taste (optional)
1 tsp sea salt
25ml water

TRY IT WITH:

+ Garlic + Thyme Chicken, Butter Bean + Sun-Dried Tomato (see page 89)
+ Steak, Sweet Potato + Rocket Salad (see page 138)

The Prawn Star
With Chipotle Caesar Dressing

Serves 2

+ Medium-Build

The love child of a Caesar salad and a prawn cocktail, this salad is fresh, light, tangy and salty, with a subtle kick that's balanced by the prawns' succulent sweetness. Serve this up ice cold for lunch, load it up between two pieces of sourdough for a killer sandwich, or pile the prawns high and you have the perfect party dish (best served with some dirty martinis and skinny fries ... apparently). If you can't find chipotle chilli flakes, finish with some smoked paprika and a sprinkling of chilli flakes for a little heat.

1. Preheat the oven to 220°C/200°C fan.
2. Drain the sweetcorn well and tip into a roasting tray. Add 2 tablespoons of olive oil and a generous pinch of sea salt. Stir to distribute evenly, and place in the oven for 15 minutes.
3. Finely chop the kale and place into a large mixing bowl. Dress with the juice of half of the lemon, a pinch of sea salt and a grind of black pepper. Use your hands to massage the dressing into the leaves to help soften and enhance flavour.
4. In a second small roasting tray, combine the prawns with the cooking salt, garlic granules and remaining 1 teaspoon of olive oil. Give the tray a shake to mix them (as much as is possible while the prawns are still frozen).
5. Once the sweetcorn's 15 minutes is up, give it a good stir with a heat-proof spoon and return to the oven.
6. Place the prawns in the oven too. Cook the prawns for 10 minutes and the corn for a further 15 minutes.
7. Meanwhile, add 2 tablespoons of Chipotle Caesar Dressing to the massaged kale, then pile it onto your serving plate. Grate over half of the Parmesan using a microplane or fine grater.
8. Slice the avocado (or chop into chunks if you prefer) and scatter over the kale.
9. Remove the prawns and then the corn from the oven. Drain the cooking liquid from the prawns, then dress them with the juice from the other half of the lemon, a good grind of pepper and a small drizzle of olive oil.
10. Scatter the roasted corn over the kale base and toss gently to mix. Next, layer on the prawns and dress with 4 tablespoons of Chipotle Caesar Dressing. Finish by grating over the remaining Parmesan and topping with your Crispy Onions and a sprinkling of chipotle chilli flakes.

---

2 x 198g tins of sweetcorn (in water)

2 tbsp + 1 tsp extra virgin olive oil, plus extra for drizzling

60g kale, destemmed, rinsed and dried

1 lemon (juice)

225g frozen raw peeled jumbo king prawns

¼ tsp fine cooking salt

¼ tsp garlic granules

40g Parmesan

1 ripe avocado

Pinch of chipotle chilli flakes

Sea salt and black pepper

READY TO ROCK:

6 tbsp Chipotle Caesar Dressing (see page 36)

3 tbsp Crispy Onions (see page 24 for home-made, or shop-bought works fine)

TIP:

Whack this in a wrap for a cracking lunch-on-the-go.

The SP Caesar

With Chipotle Caesar Dressing

Serves 2

+ Quick-Build

CREAMY

A recipe for Caesar Salad in a book all about salads is, frankly, completely unavoidable. We have the trusty Caesar to thank for keeping salads alive in the lowest moments of their history, and it's no surprise. There are few meals more perfectly balanced, or more likely to cause a bout of food envy. Here we have our classic SP Caesar, loaded with spiced chicken, juicy tomatoes and Crispy Onions, but don't stop there. Get creative and customise. Go wherever the wind takes you – just don't use iceberg lettuce, please.

1. Measure the spices, salt and ½ teaspoon of olive oil into a medium mixing bowl and stir well to combine into a paste. Add the chicken fillets and use your hands to coat until the fillets are all well dressed. Set aside at room temperature to marinate while you prepare the remaining ingredients.
2. Finely chop the kale and place into a large mixing bowl. Dress with the juice of half of the lemon, a pinch of sea salt and a grind of black pepper. Use your hands to massage the dressing into the leaves to help soften and enhance the flavour.
3. Tear the lettuce leaves from the core and add them whole to the kale, gently folding through to distribute them evenly. Add 2 tablespoons of Chipotle Caesar Dressing and use your hands to toss through.
4. Slice your tomatoes into halves and set aside.
5. Heat 1 teaspoon of olive oil in a frying pan over a high heat and add your marinated chicken fillets. Once sizzling, reduce the heat to medium–high to avoid the outsides burning. Cook for 7–8 minutes, flipping the fillets with tongs every couple of minutes, until nicely golden and cooked through. Remove from the heat and squeeze over the juice from the other half of the lemon, then finish with a sprinkle of sea salt and a drizzle of olive oil.
6. Load the dressed leaves onto a serving plate, then grate over half of the Parmesan using a microplane or fine grater. Pile on your tomatoes and half the Crispy Onions.
7. After they've had a couple of minutes to rest, slice the chicken fillets (or leave whole) and lay them onto the salad. Top with the remaining Chipotle Caesar Dressing, the remaining Crispy Onions and the grated Parmesan. Finish with a drizzle of olive oil and a hefty grind of black pepper.

For Focaccia Croutons (optional):

1. Preheat the oven to 200°C/180°C fan. Slice or tear 200g focaccia into 5–7cm pieces and place in a mixing bowl. Add 2 tablespoons olive oil and a pinch of sea salt. Use your hands to coat well, then place onto a baking tray. Bake in the oven for 10 minutes before shaking the tray and returning to the oven for a further 7 minutes until crisp and golden.

½ tsp ground cumin

½ tsp garlic granules

½ tsp paprika

½ tsp cayenne pepper

½ tsp fine cooking salt

1½ tsp extra virgin olive oil, plus extra for drizzling

425g mini chicken fillets

50g kale, destemmed, rinsed and dried

1 lemon (juice)

½ baby gem lettuce, leaves whole, rinsed and dried

100g cherry tomatoes

40g Parmesan

Sea salt and black pepper

READY TO ROCK:

6 tbsp Chipotle Caesar Dressing (see page 36)

4 tbsp Crispy Onions (see page 24 for home-made, or shop-bought works fine)

TIP:

Make it your own by adding 10 tinned anchovies and 1 tin of sweetcorn.

CREAMY

Coconutty-Curry + Lime Dressing

Dresses 4–6 salads

This dressing was created as a seasonal special, at the time of Queen Elizabeth II's Platinum Jubilee. It's an unsung hero, in my opinion, and really brightens up any salad in both colour and flavour. You can keep it a little thicker by using less coconut milk and use it as a delicious dip, or as your base for a super-fresh coronation chicken (or coronation chickpea).

1. Peel your ginger using the edge of a teaspoon and chop finely.
2. Peel and crush your garlic using the side of a knife or a garlic crusher and a little sea salt to help turn it into a smooth paste.
3. Use a knife to remove and discard the thickest parts of the coriander stems, roughly the bottom 5cm. Keep the softer stems and leaves to use for maximum flavour.
4. Place all the ingredients into your blender and blitz until smooth. Add extra salt and lime to taste. Store in an airtight jar or container in the fridge for up to 1 week.

8g fresh ginger

1 garlic clove

Small handful of fresh coriander

1 tsp ground turmeric

2 tsp medium curry powder

200ml coconut milk or coconut yoghurt

1 lime (juice), plus extra to taste (optional)

75g mango chutney

1 tbsp toasted sesame oil

¼ tsp sea salt, plus extra to taste (optional)

TRY IT WITH:

+ Paprika Chicken Thigh with Nutty Grains + Roasted Peppers (see page 96)
+ Spiced Cauliflower with Smoky Toasted Almonds + Hot Honey Labneh (see page 95)

Curry-Mango Chicken with Lime Leaf Brown Rice

With Coconutty-Curry + Lime Dressing

Serves 2

+ Medium-Build
+ Brain + Body Fuel

This salad delivers sunshine at any time and is so easy to whip up, thanks to the creamy Coconutty-Curry + Lime Dressing doubling up as a marinade for the chicken. Have a play with the temperature of the ingredients and you'll see how versatile this salad can be – a cosy grain bowl for winter with a warming chilli-crunch kick, or a cold, crisp and crunchy salad – inspired by childhood coronation chicken picnics – with a refreshing kick of lime leaf. Don't be held back by the chicken if you're plant-based – use the dressing as a marinade for paneer, tofu or some chickpeas, and you're away.

1. Measure 4 tablespoons of Coconutty-Curry + Lime Dressing into a medium mixing bowl. Add the chicken fillets and mix well to coat. Set aside to marinate for 10–15 minutes.
2. Weigh the rice into a saucepan and measure in the water. Stir through the fine sea salt. Bring the water to a boil over a medium–high heat, then place a lid on the pot (ideally a clear one so you can see if you need to add more water at any point) and reduce the temperature to medium. Allow this to simmer until the rice is cooked – roughly 25 minutes. (Simply add more water if it dries out and isn't fully cooked.)
3. Once the rice is on, heat the sesame oil in a frying pan or griddle pan over a medium–high heat. Use tongs to add the marinated chicken fillets to the pan and cook for 3–4 minutes on each side until cooked through and golden brown on the outside.
4. Meanwhile, separate the lettuce leaves, and lay them across a serving plate. Drizzle with 2 tablespoons of Coconutty Curry + Lime Dressing.
5. Slice your cucumber down the middle and use a teaspoon to scoop out the seeds. Slice across the cucumber to create half moons that are around 1–2cm thick.
6. Slice the sugar snaps in half at an angle.
7. Once the rice is cooked, drain off any remaining water. Place the lime leaves on top of one another and slice into thin strands. Fold through the cooked rice.
8. Scatter the lime leaf rice over the lettuce leaf base and top with the chopped cucumber and sugar snaps. Arrange your chicken fillets on top (you can leave these whole, or chop into halves). Drizzle with the remaining 2 tablespoons of dressing. Top with the Quick Pickled Onions, a good spooning of Crispy Chilli Oil and a generous handful of coriander leaves.

CREAMY

250g mini chicken fillets
125g short grain brown rice
500ml water
½ tsp fine cooking salt
1 tsp toasted sesame oil
1 baby gem lettuce, rinsed and dried
½ cucumber
150g sugar snap peas
3 lime leaves
Handful of fresh coriander leaves

READY TO ROCK:

8 tbsp Coconutty-Curry + Lime Dressing (see page 42)

2 tbsp Quick Pickled Onions (see page 28)

3 tbsp Crispy Chilli Oil (see page 31)

TIP:

If you want to skip the chilli kick, switch out the Crispy Chilli Oil for some toasted flaked almonds.

CREAMY

God Save the Bean
With Coconutty-Curry + Lime Dressing

Serves 2

+ Quick-Build
+ Brain + Body Fuel

A plant-based and punchy twist on coronation chicken, this was designed as one of our first seasonal specials in celebration of Queen Elizabeth II's Platinum Jubilee. We're big believers in the power of beans, and here, combined with lashings of anti-inflammatory turmeric, they really bring the best of what they have to offer. High in soluble and insoluble fibre, beans leave you feeling fuller for longer, while slowly releasing energy from their complex carbohydrates so you'll avoid the mid-afternoon slump. They're also a great source of iron, which we need to avoid exhaustion and, lest we forget, they also deliver a juicy punch of plant protein, made complete thanks to the pistachios sprinkled atop this salad. Repeat after me: 'GOD SAVE THE BEAN!'

1. Pour the butter beans into a sieve to drain and rinse well. Leave them in the sieve while you make their marinade.
2. In a medium bowl, whisk together the mango chutney, coconut yoghurt, curry powder, turmeric, mint leaves and a pinch of sea salt until well combined. Fold the beans through the sauce and finish with a squeeze of lime juice and a pinch of sea salt, if needed.
3. Trim the ends of the stems off the parsley and discard, then add the parsley and spinach to a salad bowl. Add 2 tablespoons of Coconutty-Curry + Lime Dressing and toss gently. Pour onto a serving plate.
4. Slice the avocado and place on top of and amid the leaves, followed by the fresh mango pieces. Squeeze over the juice of half the lime and toss again. Spoon the dressed coronation butter beans over the salad, then crumble over the feta and scatter with the Quick Pickled Onions.
5. Roughly chop the pistachios and scatter them over the salad, followed by 4 tablespoons of Coconutty-Curry + Lime Dressing. Pick a handful of parsley leaves and dot them over the salad to finish.

700g jar butter beans (preferably the large Spanish ones) or 2 x 400g tins chickpeas

2 tbsp mango chutney

4 tbsp coconut yoghurt

3 tsp curry powder

½ tsp ground turmeric

10 mint leaves, finely chopped

1 lime (juice)

Handful of flat leaf parsley, plus extra leaves to garnish

Large handful of spinach

1 ripe avocado

250g pre-chopped ripe mango, or 1 very ripe mango, chopped

100g feta

100g pistachios, shelled

Sea salt

READY TO ROCK:

6 tbsp Coconutty-Curry + Lime Dressing (see page 42)

4 tbsp Quick Pickled Onions (see page 28)

TIP:

Add some red rice to increase the amount of complete protein you're pulling from this bowl and boost its fuelling power.

CREAMY

Spiced Tahini + Date Molasses Dressing

Dresses 4–6 salads

It's hard to beat a creamy tahini dressing, and this one is a super-versatile staple we'd recommend having on hand at all times. An easy road out of post-work dinner-prep panics thanks to the fact it'll go with pretty much anything in your fridge. Remove the za'atar and you have a great base to play with so many other spices. After all, we're all about customisation at The Salad Project.

1. Place the tahini, date molasses, red wine vinegar, sesame oil and water into a blender and blitz until smooth. If needed, add a little extra water to loosen the mixture.
2. Now add your za'atar and sea salt. Either blitz to fully incorporate the spices, or just stir well if you'd like to keep a bit of texture in your dressing. Store in an airtight jar or container in the fridge for up to 1 week.

70g tahini
30g date molasses
20ml red wine vinegar
30ml toasted sesame oil
100ml water, plus extra if needed
1 tsp za'atar
1 tsp sea salt

TRY IT WITH:

+ Harissa Steak + Giant Couscous with Pickled Onions + Pistachios (see page 70)
+ Whole-Spice Lamb Meatballs, Preserved Lemon + Butter Bean Salad (see page 174)

Miso Chicken with Crispy Spiced Chickpeas + Pickled Cucumbers

With Spiced Tahini + Date Molasses Dressing

Serves 2

+ Medium-Build
+ Protein Power

We've used crisped-up chickpeas as a base for this bowl to make sure it's filling without weighing you down, so it's a great way to refuel and pack a protein boost at the end of the day. It's crunchy, creamy and crisp, underpinned by warm spices and pickle-y punches, which makes it one of those salads we just can't help but going back to for more, usually with our hands thanks to the baby gem boats that form naturally as you layer up. Winner, winner, tahini chicken and pickled cucumber dinner.

1. Preheat the oven to 200°C/180°C fan.
2. Drain your chickpeas and rinse under cold, running water. Tip into a roasting tray and pat dry with kitchen paper. Sprinkle with the olive oil, ras el hanout or garam masala and a generous pinch of sea salt. Shake the tray to mix until well coated. Roast in the oven for 30 minutes until crispy.
3. Meanwhile, mix the miso paste, sesame oil, a pinch of sea salt and a few grinds of pepper in a small bowl. Add the chicken thighs and coat evenly. Place the thighs into a roasting tray, then roast in the oven for 20–25 minutes until golden.
4. Finely slice your cucumber using a knife or mandolin and place in a jar or small airtight container. Add the cooking salt, sugar, dill, vinegar and water, and leave for 15 minutes to gently pickle.
5. Place the sesame seeds into a small dry pan and toast over a medium heat until golden – roughly 3–4 minutes.
6. Separate the lettuce into individual leaves, leaving each leaf whole, then spread over a serving platter. Drizzle with 2 tablespoons of Spiced Tahini + Date Molasses Dressing, and scatter over your spiced chickpeas and pickled cucumbers.
7. Cut your chicken into slices and layer on top. Drizzle with a further 2–3 tablespoons of dressing and top with the toasted sesame seeds.

- 570g jar chickpeas (preferably the large Spanish ones) or 2 400g tins
- 1 tbsp extra virgin olive oil
- 2 tsp ras el hanout or garam masala
- 1 tsp white miso paste
- 3 tsp toasted sesame oil
- 3 chicken thighs, skinless and boneless
- ½ cucumber
- 1 tsp fine cooking salt
- 1 tsp caster sugar
- Small handful of dill, chopped
- 4 tbsp white wine vinegar
- 120ml water
- 3 tbsp sesame seeds
- 1 baby gem lettuce, rinsed and dried
- Sea salt and black pepper

READY TO ROCK:

4–5 tbsp Spiced Tahini + Date Molasses Dressing (see page 46)

TIP:

Swap out chicken for feta for a vegetarian alternative.

Roasted Aubergine with Quinoa, Maple Walnuts + Pomegranate

With Spiced Tahini + Date Molasses Dressing

Serves 2

+ Medium-Build

CREAMY

More than any other dish, salads are the perfect canvas for bringing together salty and sweet. There's no end to the outrageously delicious elements you can combine in a salad – and the epic thing is you can still call it just that: a salad. Here's one that balances salt, sweet, bitter and sour. Add to that a mad variety of textures, from crunchy maple walnuts to creamy feta, and you have salad in its absolute best light. This also works beautifully with some grilled halloumi in place of the feta as a bit of a barbecue show-stealer.

1. Preheat the oven to 220°C/200°C fan.
2. Slice the aubergine into batons and place into a colander. Add ½ teaspoon of the cooking salt and use your hands to coat the aubergine. Leave the colander in the sink to allow the salt to pull out some liquid from the aubergine.
3. Measure the quinoa into a medium saucepan and add the water, plus the remaining teaspoon of fine cooking salt. Bring to a boil over a high heat, then reduce the heat to medium and allow the quinoa to simmer for 25 minutes until the water is absorbed and the quinoa is cooked through.
4. Meanwhile, mix the maple syrup, tamari or soy sauce and 1 tablespoon of the olive oil in a large bowl with 2 tablespoons of the Spiced Tahini + Date Molasses Dressing. Give the aubergine a gentle squeeze to remove any further liquid, then add it to the marinade and coat well. Arrange the marinated aubergine in a roasting tray in a single layer, sprinkle with sea salt and roast in the oven for 15 minutes.
5. Spread the bitter leaves across your serving plate.
6. When the quinoa is cooked, rinse it briefly under cold water and dress with the lemon zest and 1 tablespoon of olive oil. Spoon the dressed quinoa over the leaf base and drizzle with 2 tablespoons of Spiced Tahini + Date Molasses Dressing.
7. Slice the cucumber down the middle and use a teaspoon to scoop out the seeds. Discard the seeds, then slice the cucumber into 2cm half moons. Scatter these over the quinoa.
8. Once the aubergine has been roasting for 15 minutes, use tongs to turn the batons, then return to the oven for 5 minutes. Turn once more and cook for a further 5 minutes until the aubergine is nicely coloured. Place the aubergine over the salad and then crumble the feta, if using, over the top.
9. Drizzle over 2 further tablespoons of dressing, then sprinkle over the Maple Walnuts and pomegranate seeds. Finish with a splash of olive oil and a sprinkle of sea salt.

---

1 aubergine

1½ tsp fine cooking salt

200g mixed-colour quinoa

700ml water

1 tbsp maple syrup

1 tbsp tamari or light soy sauce

2 tbsp extra virgin olive oil, plus extra for finishing

½ radicchio, or 3–4 endives, or a leaf mix that contains some purple leaves

1 lemon (zest)

½ cucumber

100g feta (optional)

50g pomegranate seeds

Sea salt

READY TO ROCK:

6 tbsp Spiced Tahini + Date Molasses Dressing (see page 46)

2 tbsp Maple Walnuts (see page 24)

TIP:

This salad also works great with a heap of roasted Tenderstem broccoli or courgette in place of the aubergine if you want to boost your greens.

CREAMY

Sesa-Miso Dressing

Dresses 4–6 salads

It's a non-negotiable for us to have some of this kicking about as a silky drizzle for salmon, a dressing for mushrooms or a sauce for some soba noodles. These are all ten-minute dinners that really fuelled us through the early (long) days of The Salad Project, which ultimately inspired this book!

1. Place your sesame seeds into a dry pan and place over a medium heat, swirling the pan constantly, until they are nice and toasted – about 3–4 minutes. Set aside.
2. Peel your ginger using the edge of a teaspoon and grate into a blender. Add the remaining ingredients, excluding your toasted sesame seeds, and blitz until smooth. You can also just pop all your ingredients into a jar and give it a good shake if you don't mind a bit of texture from the ginger.
3. Finish by stirring through your toasted sesame seeds and adjusting the texture with a little extra water, if needed – but I'd recommend keeping this dressing on the thicker side, in case you want to use it as a noodle sauce. Store in an airtight jar or container in the fridge for up to 1 week.

20g sesame seeds (black add lovely colour, but white are great, too)

10g fresh ginger

80g tahini

30g white miso paste

40ml rice wine vinegar

40ml tamari or light soy sauce

80ml water, plus extra if needed

TRY IT WITH:

+ Miso Salmon (see page 193)
+ Cold Soba Noodles with Kimchi, Pickled Cucumbers + Sesame Tenderstem (see page 157)
+ Roasted Aubergine, Spicy Cashew Chickpeas + Kale (see page 178)

Sesame Soy Steak with Furikake Croutons + Pickled Chillies

With Sesa-Miso Dressing

Serves 2

+ Medium-Build
+ Protein Power

GF / CREAMY

We love the combination of textures in this salad. It's piled with tons of great crunch, but sometimes crunches that aren't backed up with some more filling body can leave you feeling a little hungry. That's why we've added some nutty brown rice, which soaks up the creamy sesame dressing so damn well. Pickled chillies bring some real zing, as does the steak's salty marinade. Oof. Cooking this with two steaks makes it hearty enough to replace your usual steak night, but for a light dinner for two, just one steak should be enough.

1. Preheat the oven to 220°C/200°C fan.
2. Peel and crush your garlic, using the side of a knife or a garlic crusher to turn it into a smooth paste.
3. Place the crushed garlic, oyster sauce, 2 teaspoons of the sesame oil and the tamari or soy sauce into a shallow dish or plastic container and whisk to combine. Add your steaks and cover well on both sides. Set aside for 10–15 minutes to come to room temperature.
4. Weigh the rice into a saucepan and measure in the water. Stir through the fine cooking salt. Bring the water to a boil over a medium–high heat, then place a lid on the pot (ideally a clear one so you can see if you need to add more water at any point) and lower the temperature to medium. Allow this to simmer until the rice is cooked – roughly 25 minutes. (Simply add more water if it dries out and isn't fully cooked.)
5. Slice your bread of choice into chunky croutons and place in a roasting tray. Add the remaining 2 tablespoons of sesame oil, a generous pinch of sea salt and 2 teaspoons of the furikake seasoning. Mix well until your croutons are nicely coated. Pop into the oven for 5 minutes, give them a shake, then return to the oven for a further 5 minutes until nicely golden and crunchy (if using bao buns, toast for 3–4 minutes total).
6. Meanwhile, place your green beans in a sieve and pop it beneath the lid of your rice pot while the rice is still cooking to steam the beans for 2–3 minutes. Remove and run under cold water to stop the cooking, then set aside.
7. Top and tail the radishes and cut into halves or quarters, depending on their size. Place in a bowl of cold water to crisp up.
8. Now all your vegetables and croutons are ready, heat a dry frying pan over a high heat. Once really nice and hot, use tongs to place your steaks into the pan, pressing down for a second to help them caramelise. Leave the steaks to cook on one side for 3 minutes before flipping over for rare, or

1 garlic clove
1 tbsp oyster sauce
2 tbsp + 2 tsp toasted sesame oil
80ml tamari (for gluten-free) or light soy sauce
2 beef rump steaks
125g short grain brown rice
500ml water
½ tsp fine cooking salt
125g sourdough (stale or fresh) or bao buns
3 tsp furikake seasoning
100g green beans, ends trimmed
120g radishes
Handful of pea shoots, watercress or rocket
Handful of fresh coriander leaves
1 lime (juice)
Sea salt

READY TO ROCK:

6 tbsp Sesa-Miso Dressing (see page 28)

2 tbsp Pickled Chillies (see page 52)

5 minutes if you would like them medium. Spoon a couple of teaspoons of the leftover marinade over the steaks and cook for a further 3 minutes for a rare steak, 5 minutes for medium Remove from the pan and drape over an upside-down cereal bowl on a lipped plate (to allow the juices to run out without them going everywhere). Allow both steaks to rest for at least 10 minutes before slicing.

9. While they rest, cover your serving platter or plates with pea shoots, watercress or rocket, and gently spoon over your rice. Sprinkle over the green beans, radishes and half of the croutons. Dress with 3 tablespoons of Sesa-Miso Dressing.

10. Slice your steaks into 2cm-thick slices, going against the grain of the meat. Sprinkle the slices with the remaining 1 teaspoon of furikake seasoning. Lie your steak slices over your salad and top with the remaining croutons and the Pickled Chillies. Finish with some coriander leaves, the lime juice and another 3 tablespoons of your Sesa-Miso Dressing.

TIP: MAKE IT PLANT-BASED

Chop 250g super-firm tofu and place onto a parchment-lined roasting tray with a pinch of sea salt, black pepper and a generous drizzle of olive oil. Roast at 200°C/180°C fan for 20 minutes, shaking the tray after 10 minutes. Mix together 2 tablespoons Sesa-Miso Dressing, 1 tablespoon tamari or light soy sauce and 1 tablespoon Crispy Chilli Oil or 1 tablespoon toasted sesame oil. Remove the tofu from the oven, add the sauce to the tray and toss the tofu in it to dress. Serve in place of steak.

Chilled Sesame Noodles with Balsamic Mushrooms, Lime Slaw + Toasted Furikake Seeds

With Sesa-Miso Dressing

Serves 2
+ Quick-Build
+ Gut Happy

CREAMY

Noodle salads are one of the greatest gifts to home cooks who are time-poor. With quick-cook noodles ready in two minutes, we're always shocked by how fast you can whip up something nutrient-dense that packs a flavour punch. This is a cold bowl of umami flavour pops that will recharge your batteries, while reserving your energy thanks to the minimal effort it requires. It's also a great base recipe to get creative with – mix-and-match the dressing, toppings and crunch, serve hot or cold, and even loosen out the drizzle with coconut milk for an energising noodle soup. Always keep some quick-cook noodles to hand – you never know when your batteries might run low.

1. Preheat the oven to 220°C/200°C fan and boil the kettle.
2. Place the udon noodles into a heat-proof bowl, then cover with boiling water. Let the noodles sit for 2 minutes, then use tongs to agitate them into individual strands. Drain off the hot water and either place the noodles in a bowl of iced water, or rinse with cold water to cool.
3. Place the vinegar, tamari or soy sauce, sesame oil and sesame seeds into a large mixing bowl and whisk together. Rinse any dirt off the mushrooms, then tear or chop the largest ones in half. Keep any smaller ones whole, and remember they will shrink in the oven, so, if in doubt, leave them whole. Add the mushrooms to the bowl of marinade and use your hands to mix them well in order to coat, ensuring the sesame seeds are evenly distributed. Transfer to a parchment-lined roasting tray and place in the oven for 18 minutes.
4. While the mushrooms are cooking, thinly slice your red cabbage using a sharp knife, a mandolin or a vegetable peeler. Place into a bowl and dress with the juice of half the lime and the pinch of sea salt. Mix well with your hands until the cabbage is well coated and starting to soften.
5. Add 6 tablespoons of Sesa-Miso Dressing to the cooked and cooled udon noodles and pour onto your serving dish. Add the limey cabbage slaw, kimchi and cooked mushrooms, making sure you include all the juices and sesame seeds left on the tray after cooking. Add Sesa-Miso Dressing and the juice of the other half of the lime. Top with the Toasted Furikake Seeds and a small handful of coriander leaves.

Ingredients
2 x 200g sachets pre-cooked udon noodles
4 tbsp balsamic vinegar
2 tbsp tamari or light soy sauce
2 tbsp toasted sesame oil
1 tbsp sesame seeds
240g shiitake mushrooms or chestnut mushrooms
150g red cabbage
1 lime (juice)
1 pinch of sea salt
3 tbsp kimchi (optional)
Small handful of fresh coriander leaves

READY TO ROCK:

8 tbsp Sesa-Miso Dressing (see page 52)

2 tbsp Toasted Furikake Seeds (see page 25)

TIP:

Add a jammy egg to boost the protein of this bowl. Prepare a bowl of iced water. Boil some salted water and carefully drop in 1–2 eggs. Leave to cook for 6.5 minutes before moving to the iced water to cool completely. Peel, halve and lay on top of your mushrooms.

CREAMY

Coconut Ranch Dressing

Dresses 4–6 salads

This is a healthy (and optionally vegan) twist on a classic mayonnaise-based dressing that we like to put in the same camp as a Caesar: creamy, garlicky and completely unavoidable when you get a craving for a slightly naughty, ice cold and crunchy salad (and maybe a side of chips).

1. Finely chop your shallot (or roughly chop if you're going to blitz the dressing in a blender).
2. Peel and crush your garlic using the side of a knife or a garlic crusher and a little sea salt to help turn it into a smooth paste.
3. Chop the thicker ends off your herbs (2–3cm) and discard. If you're hand-whisking, chop your herbs finely. If using a blender, they are fine as they are.
4. Place all the ingredients into a blender, if using, and blitz until almost smooth, if you'd like some texture from the herbs, or totally smooth if you prefer. Alternatively, just whisk all the ingredients together for a chunkier ranch.
5. Adjust the salt and pepper to taste. Store in an airtight jar or container in the fridge for up to 1 week.

1 shallot
1 garlic clove
Small handful of flat leaf parsley
Small handful of chives
Small handful of basil
Small handful of dill
150ml coconut yoghurt or coconut milk
1 tbsp apple cider vinegar
60g mayonnaise (plant-based if vegan)
2 tsp sea salt
1 tsp black pepper

TRY IT WITH:

+ Honey Chicken + Jalapeño Quinoa Salad with Toasted Pine Nuts + Tenderstem (see page 148)
+ Mex on the Beach (see page 188)
+ Hot Honey Halloumi + Dill Fattoush (see page 86)

Potato Salad with Smoked Bacon + Shredded Roast Chicken

With Coconut Ranch Dressing

Serves 2

+ Medium-Build

CREAMY

Salads are often overlooked when we think of comfort food, but this is exactly that. A crowd-pleaser for some al fresco summer dining, or just a dinner for two that you'll want to load into a bowl and eat on the sofa. And you can lick it all up in the knowledge you're consuming more than 10 plants in one go. Welcome to the new era of comfort eating with your Salad Project.

1. Preheat the oven to 220°C/200°C fan.
2. Rinse and chop the potatoes into halves or thirds. Place in a saucepan, cover with water and add 1 teaspoon of the cooking salt. Bring to a boil, then reduce the heat to low and simmer the potatoes for around 15 minutes, until a skewer passes into them without resistance.
3. While the potatoes are boiling, use a medium mixing bowl to mix the garlic granules, oregano, a good grind of pepper and the remaining ½ teaspoon of cooking salt with the olive oil. Add the chicken breasts and coat them well in the marinade. Leave to sit for 10 minutes at room temperature.
4. While the chicken sits, place the lardons in a small frying pan over a medium heat and allow the fat to render, then the bacon to crisp up – 4–5 minutes. Place the crispy bacon lardons onto some kitchen paper to soak up excess oil.
5. Place the chicken breasts into a roasting tray and roast in the oven for 20 minutes.
6. Start building the salad while the chicken cooks. Place your potatoes and bacon into a mixing bowl and add 4 tablespoons of Coconut Ranch Dressing, plus a pinch of sea salt and a grind of pepper.
7. Chop the roots of the endives or chicory and pull their leaves apart, keeping them whole. Spread them over your serving plate.
8. Cut the avocado into generous chunks and scatter over the leaves. Dress with 2 tablespoons of Coconut Ranch Dressing, then layer on the potato and bacon mix.
9. Finely chop the spring onions and chives and set aside.
10. Once the chicken is cooked, slice with a knife or shred it with 2 forks and arrange over the potatoes. Top the chicken with 2 more tablespoons of the Coconut Ranch Dressing and sprinkle the whole salad generously with your chives and spring onions.

500g new potatoes

1½ tsp fine cooking salt

1 tsp garlic granules

1 tsp dried oregano

2 tbsp extra virgin olive oil

2 chicken breasts

80g smoked bacon lardons

2 endives or chicory

1 ripe avocado

2 spring onions

4 chive stems

Sea salt and black pepper

READY TO ROCK:

8 tbsp Coconut Ranch Dressing (see page 58)

TIP:

This is a great way to use up leftover roast chicken – shred it into the dressing and use as a topping for a roast sweet potato in its jacket if you're looking for something a little more nutrient-dense.

CREAMY

Roasted Corn + Red Beans with Crispy Onions + Feta

With Coconut Ranch Dressing

Serves 2

+ Quick-Build

When testing recipes for this book, this came out as one of our surprise favourites. It's the perfect example of how the best salads can be simple, simple, simple. Whipped up from some arguably unsexy leftovers kicking about the kitchen, each ingredient gets the little touch of love it needs so when they are layered together, you get something seriously sexy. Seek out the really great-quality jarred red kidney beans we're lucky enough to be able to access pretty easily these days – their flavour, enhanced with a juicy lime squeeze, provides an epic base to this build. As it stands, this makes for a zingy lunch – or you can shovel it into warm tortillas for a more filling dinner (because the sexiest salads should, as a rule, be eaten in the least sexy way).

1. Preheat the oven to 220°C/200°C fan.
2. Place your drained sweetcorn into a medium roasting tray. Add the olive oil and a pinch of sea salt, and stir through the corn to coat it with seasoning. Roast the corn for 15 minutes, then stir and return to the oven for a further 15 minutes until well coloured.
3. Pour the red kidney beans onto your serving dish, then grate over the lime zest. Squeeze half of the lime's juice over the beans and season with a pinch of sea salt. Drizzle 2 tablespoons of Coconut Ranch Dressing over the beans.
4. Cut your avocado into large chunks and arrange over the dish.
5. Pick the coriander leaves off the stems and scatter over the dish, reserving some to garnish. Scatter over the roasted corn, then layer on your Pickled Chillies. Crumble the feta across the salad, if using, and add 3 more tablespoons of the Coconut Ranch Dressing. Top with the Crispy Onions, some final coriander leaves and the Tajín seasoning.

2 x 198g tins of sweetcorn (in water), drained
2 tbsp extra virgin olive oil
700g jar red kidney beans or 2 x 400g tins, drained and rinsed
1 lime (zest of whole, juice of half)
1 ripe avocado
Large handful of fresh coriander
200g feta (optional)
1 tsp Tajín seasoning (or a pinch of sea salt, some chilli flakes and some extra lime zest)
Sea salt

READY TO ROCK:

5 tbsp Coconut Ranch Dressing (see page 58)
1 tbsp Pickled Chillies (see page 28)
1 tbsp Crispy Onions (see page 24 for home-made, or shop-bought works fine)

TIP:

Load up the protein with some spiced chicken thighs or garlic and lime prawns. If you're plant-based and want to up the protein, add some brown rice to make your beans a complete protein source.

CREAMY

Whipped Feta + Dill Drizzle

Dresses 4–6 salads

This is a recipe that epitomises why we set out to write this book: to show that there is more to dressings than crusty, back-of-fridge mustard and vinegar whisked up with some olive oil. Silky smooth feta ready to step in as a drizzle, dressing or dip at a moment's notice. A great way to use up the half-block of feta left over from last night's dinner – and in a particularly eye-catching shade of SP green, what's not to love?

Small handful of dill

100g feta

120g extra virgin olive oil

1 lemon (juice)

2 tsp runny honey

2 ice cubes

1. Remove the coarser ends of the dill stems and discard, then roughly chop the rest and place in a blender.
2. Crumble in your feta and add the olive oil, lemon juice, honey and ice cubes (these stop the feta from melting in the heat of the blending process and save the dressing from splitting). Blitz on the highest speed for 2–3 minutes until completely, silky smooth. Store in an airtight container for up to 1 week (just give it a stir before use if it starts to separate).

TRY IT WITH:

+ Green 'n' Minty Whole Grain Pasta Salad (see page 143)
+ Steak, Sweet Potato + Rocket Salad (see page 138)

TIP

Place in the fridge to chill and thicken, and serve drizzled with olive oil and honey as an excellent dip for ice-cold crudités and crisps.

Beetroot + Chorizo with Hot Honey + Toasted Buckwheat

With Whipped Feta + Dill Drizzle

Serves 2

+ Quick-Build

CREAMY

This is a great salad for when you're feeling a little bit fancy, but don't want too much faff. Honey, chorizo and sweet pickled beetroot are a killer combination, while crunchy toasted buckwheat is a great way of adding some texture and takes just a few minutes in a frying pan – one to keep up your sleeve if you need some crunch in future.

1. Gently heat a dry frying pan over a medium heat, then add the green buckwheat groats, 1 tablespoon of the olive oil, a pinch of sea salt and the smoked paprika. Stir to coat the buckwheat, then continue stirring regularly for 3–4 minutes until the groats have turned a deep golden. Set aside on a plate to cool, but keep the pan to hand.
2. Weigh the couscous into a saucepan, then add the water and vegetable stock jelly or cube. Bring to a boil over a high heat, then slightly reduce the heat and simmer for 6 minutes. Drain the liquid and rinse the couscous with cold water to slightly cool and avoid it sticking. Add the remaining 1 tablespoon of olive oil and a pinch of salt and stir.
3. Slice the chorizo into 1cm coins or chop into cubes. Cook the chorizo in the frying pan you used before over a low–medium heat to allow the oil to render and the sausage to crisp up without quickly burning. Once nice and crispy, set the pan aside.
4. Dollop and spread 5 tablespoons of the Whipped Feta + Dill Drizzle over the bottom of the serving plate.
5. Chop the beetroot into generous chunks, then dot the beetroot and couscous over the dressing base.
6. Next, take your dill and remove and discard the bottom 5cm of the stems, then lay it over and around the couscous, reserving a few sprigs to garnish. Layer on the chorizo and any oils from the pan, along with 2–3 tablespoons of the Whipped Feta + Dill Drizzle. Sprinkle over your toasted buckwheat and some final sprigs of dill. If using, drizzle the salad with some Hot Honey and serve while the chorizo is still warm.

80g green buckwheat groats

2 tbsp extra virgin olive oil

Pinch of smoked paprika

200g giant couscous

1 litre water

1 vegetable stock jelly or 1 cube

150g chorizo (mild or spicy)

300g pack of beetroot in vinegar

Small handful of dill

Sea salt

READY TO ROCK:

7–8 tbsp Whipped Feta + Dill Drizzle (see page 62)

2 tbsp Hot Honey (optional) (see page 31)

TIP:

Make sure you buy raw/green buckwheat, instead of 'toasted buckwheat'. The latter is extremely hard and you'll find yourself worried about cracking a tooth ... green buckwheat is softer and takes on the texture of chopped nuts once cooked using this method.

CREAMY

Tomatoes on Toast with Minty Courgette Ribbons + Capers

With Whipped Feta + Dill Drizzle

Serves 2

+ Quick-Build

Consider this our take on a piled-up panzanella that makes for a great dinner if you have some sourdough that's about to go stale and fancy something with a bit of crunch. If you're not a fan of sourdough, this also works on rye bread or, better yet, some thinly sliced focaccia. It's a quick, fuss-free recipe you can enjoy eating with your hands while closing your eyes and thinking of Italy (although Italians would kill us for suggesting this was anything close to a panzanella).

1. Preheat the oven to 220°C/200°C fan.
2. Slice your tomatoes into halves and lay, cut side up, in a single layer on a roasting tray. Drizzle with the balsamic vinegar, 1 tablespoon of the olive oil and a pinch of sea salt. Whack into the oven to roast for 10 minutes until golden and blistering.
3. Meanwhile, place your sourdough slices into a separate tray, drizzle both sides with olive oil and sprinkle with sea salt, then scatter your olives and capers around the edges of the tray. Pop this into the oven for 20 minutes, turning the bread halfway through.
4. While your tomatoes are roasting, use a peeler to peel large ribbons of the courgettes into a bowl. Add 2 pinches of sea salt, and leave to sit for 10 minutes while the salt draws out moisture. Give the courgettes a good squeeze to remove any liquid. Discard the liquid, then place the ribbons back in the bowl.
5. Finely chop the mint leaves and add them, plus 1 teaspoon of the olive oil and a grind of black pepper, to the courgettes. Fold to mix.
6. To assemble, place the sourdough slices onto a serving plate, leaving the capers and olives aside for a minute. Spread 1 tablespoon of Whipped Feta + Dill Drizzle over each slice, then pile a small handful of rocket onto each. Spoon over the tomatoes, making sure you scoop up any juice from the tray. Place your courgette ribbons over the top and dress with 4 more tablespoons of the Whipped Feta + Dill Drizzle. Top with the roasted capers and olives and a final drizzle of olive oil.

300g cherry or baby plum tomatoes

1 tbsp balsamic vinegar

1 tbsp + 1 tsp extra virgin olive oil, plus extra for drizzling

4 slices of sourdough bread

50g Kalamata olives

30g capers, drained

2 courgettes

5 sprigs of mint, leaves picked

60g rocket

Sea salt and black pepper

READY TO ROCK:

6 tbsp Whipped Feta + Dill Drizzle (see page 62)

TIP:

You can also serve this as a salad in its classic sense, by slicing the bread into croutons before toasting in the oven with the capers and olives, and covering your serving plate in uncooked tomato halves, folded through with the roasted tomatoes and courgette ribbons.

Tahini + Preserved Lemon Dressing

Dresses 4–6 salads

Tahini-lemon dressings are a little overdone in our opinion, and usually miss the mark when it comes to packing enough of a flavour punch that good salads need. We've swapped in preserved lemon instead, because it's the killer combo of both salt and acid in one. And, in conjunction with citrusy sumac, it shocks this old classic with a lightning bolt of lemon, giving it a new lease of life.

1. Peel and crush your garlic using the side of a knife or a garlic crusher and a little sea salt to help turn it into a smooth paste.
2. Finely chop the preserved lemon, removing any pips that pop out in the process. Add the chopped lemon and the tablespoon of its brine to a high-speed blender, along with the garlic, tahini, mirin, sesame oil, sumac and salt, and blitz until smooth. Stir in the water bit by bit until you're happy with the texture of your dressing.
3. Add extra salt and sumac to taste. Store in an airtight jar or container in the fridge for up to 1 week.

2 garlic cloves

1 preserved lemon, plus 1 tbsp of its brine

40g tahini

2 tbsp mirin

2 tbsp toasted sesame oil

½ tsp sumac, plus extra to taste (optional)

1 tsp sea salt, plus extra to taste (optional)

80ml water

CREAMY

TRY IT WITH:

+ Roasted Aubergine with Quinoa, Maple Walnuts + Pomegranate (see page 49)
+ Crispy Spiced Lamb, Aubergine + Freekeh with Pickled Onions (see page 100)

Sumac Salmon with Honey Carrots, Roasted Tenderstem + Lemony Grains

With Tahini + Preserved Lemon Dressing

Serves 2

+ Quick-Build
+ Brain + Body Fuel

CREAMY

A seriously hearty, healthy and colourful salad, this is a go-to for providing your body and mind with some love. From roasted salmon – which promotes brain health – and bulgur wheat – which delivers slow-release energy, helping avoid blood-sugar spikes – to the super-spice sumac – which aids with nutrient absorption, digestion, immunity and skin health – this is the poster girl for demonstrating just how much goodness can be squeezed into one salad. Fortunately, it's also tantalisingly tasty thanks to the balance of subtly sweet carrots, nutty grains, zingy pomegranate seeds and tongue-tingling fresh mint. Do your mind and body a favour.

1. Preheat the oven to 220°C/200°C fan and boil the kettle.
2. Chop the tops off the baby carrots, then place into a roasting tin with 2 tablespoons of the olive oil and a generous pinch of sea salt. Place into the oven for 10 minutes.
3. Meanwhile, cook the bulgur wheat or freekeh with the lentils and stock jelly or cube according to the packet instructions. Drain once cooked.
4. After 10 minutes, remove the carrots from the oven, then add the honey and give the carrots a shake. Return to the oven for a further 5 minutes.
5. Now line a roasting tray with parchment paper and place your salmon fillets into the middle. Sprinkle each with 1 teaspoon of sumac. Surround the salmon with the broccoli, then drizzle with olive oil and sprinkle with sea salt. Make use of the Tip on the right if you've got a little time to spare. Place into the oven for 12 minutes.
6. Meanwhile, check the bulgur wheat and lentils to see if they're soft and cooked through (you still want a little bite!). Drain the grains through a sieve to remove any excess liquid, then pour into a mixing bowl. Add 1 tablespoon of the olive oil, along with the lemon zest and juice. Fold through the chopped mint leaves.
7. Now it's time to build. Cover your serving plate with the minty bulgur wheat and lentils, and layer on the roasted broccoli. Drizzle with 3 tablespoons of Tahini + Preserved Lemon Dressing. Add the honey carrots and then either lay the salmon fillets on top whole, or use a fork to flake the salmon flesh over the salad. Discard the skin if you're not using the Tip. Finish with 3 tablespoons of Tahini + Preserved Lemon Dressing, along with the pomegranate seeds and a final sprinkle of sumac.

200g baby carrots

3 tbsp extra virgin olive oil, plus extra for drizzling

150g coarse bulgur wheat or freekeh

50g dried brown or green lentils

½ vegetable stock jelly or ½ cube

2 tsp runny honey

2 salmon fillets

2 tsp sumac, plus extra for sprinkling

150g Tenderstem broccoli or regular broccoli

1 lemon (zest of whole, juice of half)

5 sprigs of mint, leaves picked and roughly chopped

2 tbsp pomegranate seeds

Sea salt and black pepper

READY TO ROCK:

6 tbsp Tahini + Preserved Dressing (see page 68)

TIP:

To get the most from the healthy fats in your salmon, make use of the skin. Season the salmon all over with sumac and a little sea salt, then drizzle the skin with olive oil and fry over a medium-high heat, skin side down, until crisp and golden, then pop the fish, skin side up, into the oven.

Harissa Steak + Giant Couscous with Pickled Onions + Pistachios

With Tahini + Preserved Lemon Dressing

Serves 2

+ Quick-Build

We like people who think about achieving the greatest impact as efficiently as possible. This is date-night dinner for those people. Steak and pistachios certainly aren't everyday ingredients, but if you've decided to go for it, don't give up your whole evening to complicated instructions and hours of cooking. This North African-inspired salad is bright, fresh and balanced, and it's ready in just 20 minutes. Pistachios are also one of the most protein-dense nuts out there, so combined with some steak, this is a great way to recover from an intense week of movement without expending much energy.

1. Place the rose harissa into a shallow dish or plastic container. Add the steak(s) and coat well in the harissa, then rub a generous pinch of sea salt and a few grinds of pepper into each side. Leave to come to room temperature for 10–15 minutes.
2. Weigh the giant couscous into a saucepan and add the vegetable stock and water. Bring to a boil over a high heat, then reduce the heat to medium to simmer the couscous for 6 minutes, or until cooked through. Pour into a sieve to drain and rinse with cold water to cool. Place into a mixing bowl with the olive oil, lemon zest and chopped parsley. Mix until evenly distributed.
3. Cover your serving plate with pea shoots (reserving a few sprigs to garnish) or rocket, then scatter with couscous. Drizzle with 2 tablespoons of the Tahini + Preserved Lemon Dressing.
4. Place a dry, shallow frying pan over a high heat until very hot (you can test by splashing a tiny amount of water into the pan and seeing if it sizzles). Use tongs to place your steak(s) into the hot pan and press down to avoid curling and encourage caramelisation. Don't move the steak(s) for 3 minutes for rare, 5 minutes for medium, then flip and leave to caramelise on the other side for a further 3 minutes for rare, 5 minutes for medium. Remove from the pan and drape over an upside-down cereal bowl on a lipped plate (to allow the juices to run out without them going everywhere). Leave to rest for a minimum of 10 minutes.
5. Meanwhile, shell and roughly chop your pistachios, then scatter half over the couscous.
6. Once rested, slice your steak by cutting against the grain and arrange over the salad. Spoon your Quick Pickled Onions over the top, drizzle with 3–4 tablespoons of Tahini + Preserved Lemon Dressing, then top with the remaining pistachios and some extra pea shoots, if using.

2–4 tbsp rose harissa (4 tbsp if using 2 steaks)

1–2 fillet or rump steak(s)

150g giant wholewheat couscous

½ vegetable stock jelly or ½ cube

500ml water

1 tbsp extra virgin olive oil

1 lemon (zest)

Small handful of flat leaf parsley, chopped

Handful of pea shoots or rocket

100g pistachios

Sea salt and black pepper

READY TO ROCK:

5–6 tbsp Tahini + Preserved Lemon Dressing (see page 68)

2 tbsp Quick Pickled Onions (see page 28)

TIP:

Turn this into a great sandwich or open sandwich by grabbing some focaccia or ciabatta, slicing it in half, toasting it and spreading with some extra harissa. Layer in the salad greens, pistachios and sliced steak and dress generously with your dressing.

Zingy
72–113

Zingy dressings have the potential to pack a serious punch, serving up an eye-watering burst of acidity with every bite. It is easy to underestimate what it takes to turn a lettuce leaf into something we keep reaching back to for more, so this section spotlights the dressings that stand up for themselves in the simplest of salads – the underdogs of The Salad Project dressing section.

The common denominator for the dressings in this chapter is, of course, their ability to deliver zing. By 'zing', we mean tongue-tingling freshness, that sting of crisp acidity that leaves you feeling lighter after eating than before you started (but never hungry, we promise).

Zing brings flair to the most boring of salads (not that we'd know anything about those), and is an efficient way to whip up something fresh, healthy and energising in minutes (something we know a lot about).

It is the various acids that bring major zing to these recipes – so have a play with different vinegars and citrus fruits to customise yours once you've got to grips with the basics.

KEY CHARACTERISTIC:

Tongue-tingling acidity

BEST WHEN:

Shaken up by hand
(with a few exceptions)

BUILD YOUR OWN

Curate your own zingy combinations with this simple formula:

SALT   ACID   FAT   SWEET

Zingy dressings are all about acid, so playing with these ingredients is how you can get creative.

ZING TO EXPERIMENT WITH:

+ Red wine vinegar
+ White wine vinegar
+ Apple cider vinegar
+ Balsamic vinegar
+ Rice wine vinegar
+ Lemons
+ Limes

DOS AND DON'TS FOR ZINGY DRESSINGS:

+ The best way to taste whether your dressing packs enough punch is to dip a lettuce leaf in it and give it a taste – that way, you'll see how well the flavour clings to your salad.
+ A sure-fire way to dilute your vinaigrette's power is with water – make sure your leaves are dry before dressing.
+ Zingy dressings and vinaigrettes can drown a salad if overused – add them bit by bit and at the last minute before serving.
+ Avoid blending vinaigrettes if you want to keep them light and fresh – when blended, they can emulsify into a thick, claggy dressing.
+ Zingy dressings can be delicious when slightly warmed – give it a go with Apple Cider Vinaigrette (see page 76) and Brown Butter + Miso Vinaigrette (see page 110).
+ With their thinner, glossy texture, vinaigrettes make a great option for dressing up your grains after cooking.
+ Zingy dressings are great with a little texture, so keep some bite with herbs, wholegrain mustard and whole cracked spices.
+ Make use of honey, sugar or agave to temper too much salt and acidity.

Apple Cider Vinaigrette

Dresses 4–6 salads

When writing a book of salad dressings, we couldn't omit the classics – even if they are used disproportionately often compared to other, more exciting options! An apple cider vinaigrette, when done well, crowns the category of 'zing' with immense success – just don't forget to use only the best-quality ingredients for optimum health and optimum flavour. This vinaigrette is a gut-health and good-flavour powerhouse that should have a permanent spot in your fridge given its versatility and vibrancy. Just be sure to follow the jar-and-shake method. Remember: a blender has no place near this vinaigrette.

70ml apple cider vinegar

2 tsp Dijon mustard

2 tsp wholegrain mustard

1 tsp runny honey or soft light brown sugar

140ml extra virgin olive oil

½ tsp sea salt, plus extra to taste (optional)

1. Take a jam jar and measure in all of your ingredients. Close the lid tightly and shake vigorously to create a smooth vinaigrette.
2. Taste by dipping a lettuce leaf (or just a spoon) into the vinaigrette and tasting. Add salt if needed. Store in an airtight jar or container in the fridge for up to 1 week and shake before each use.

TRY IT WITH:

+ A Spoonful of Goodness Salad (see page 108)
+ Honey Chicken + Jalapeño Quinoa Salad with Toasted Pine Nuts + Tenderstem (see page 148)
+ Salty-and-Sweet Cavolo Nero, Quinoa + Black Cherry Salad with Blue Cheese + Maple Walnuts (see page 171)
+ Tuna Steak Niçoise + Jammy Eggs (see page 106)

Pork Mì

With Apple Cider Vinaigrette

Serves 2

+ Long-Build

Pork belly and salad aren't two elements that have a long-standing history, but we're in the game of redefining salads, so we developed a deliciously vibrant, light and zingy salad that balances a tingly vinaigrette with a sticky, caramelised Vietnamese-style pork belly. It's so easy to cook this pork to perfection in just 30 minutes, but the base of this salad is also incredibly versatile. You can sub in tofu and omit the fish sauce if you're looking for something plant-based.

1. Preheat the oven to 220°C/200°C fan.
2. Into a mixing bowl, measure the brown sugar, sriracha, tamari or soy sauce, fish sauce, the juice of 1 lime and the sesame oil. Peel the ginger using the edge of a teaspoon and then use a microplane to grate it (or chop and crush it with a knife), then add to the mixing bowl. Add the pork cubes to the marinade and coat well. Leave to sit for 5 minutes.
3. Meanwhile, shred the cabbage very finely, using a knife or a mandolin, and place into a mixing bowl with the juice of 1 lime and the fine cooking salt. Use your hands or a spoon to mix well to help the salt dissolve.
4. Place the pork into a roasting tray that allows it to comfortably sit in one layer, but isn't so massive the pork only takes up a small corner of the tray. Place in the oven for 20 minutes.
5. Finely chop your cos lettuce, rinse and dry, then pile it up on a serving plate.
6. If your edamame beans are frozen, bring a saucepan of water to a boil and add the beans. Cook for 3 minutes before draining and running under cold water for 60 seconds to keep their colour (you can also put the drained beans into a bowl of iced water, if easier).
7. Adding 1 tablespoon at a time to avoid overdressing, dress the leaves and edamame beans with 2 tablespoons of Apple Cider Vinaigrette and gently toss. Evenly spread the lime slaw over the lettuce base, then sprinkle over your Pickled Chillies or fresh chillies and Toasted Furikake Seeds or toasted sesame or pumpkin seeds, saving a few to garnish.
8. Once the pork has been cooking for 20 minutes, use a spoon or wooden spatula to turn the pork over and pull in any of the caramelised juices from the corners of the pan so the meat gets a good coating in the sticky sauce. Return to the oven for another 8–10 minutes until sticky, dark and caramelised. Place the pork over the salad and top with another 2–3 tablespoons of Apple Cider Vinaigrette, then finish with the reserved Pickled Chillies or fresh chillies and seeds.

---

2 tbsp soft dark brown sugar

1 tbsp sriracha

1 tsp tamari (for gluten-free) or light soy sauce

1 tsp fish sauce

2 limes (juice)

2 tsp toasted sesame oil

10g fresh ginger

350g pork belly, cut into 7cm dice

¼ red cabbage

¼ tsp fine cooking salt

½–1 cos lettuce

100g edamame beans (fresh or frozen)

READY TO ROCK:

4–5 tbsp Apple Cider Vinaigrette (see page 76)

3 tbsp Pickled Chillies (see page 28) or freshly sliced chilli

4 tbsp Toasted Furikake Seeds (see page 25) or toasted pumpkin or sesame seeds

TIP:

Swap out the pork for a couple of tuna steaks. Just marinate the steaks, then sear in a hot pan for 30 seconds on each side, before adding the leftover marinade and allowing it to caramelise in the pan with the tuna for 60 seconds or so.

Green + Crunch
With Apple Cider Vinaigrette

Serves 2

+ Quick-Build
+ Brain + Body Fuel

There's always a temptation to design a salad around a centrepiece ingredient, but sometimes you can't beat just chucking in a little bit of everything. We love this salad because it's filled with lots of pockets of goodness, from charred broccoli to pops of creamy goat's cheese. Toasted Furikake Seeds and Paprika Almonds pack the punch when it comes to the nutritional value of this recipe, so think of this as a brain-loving bowl that'll be kind to your mind, skin and tummy (thanks to the gut-loving Apple Cider Vinaigrette).

1. Preheat the oven to 220°C/200°C fan.
2. If your edamame beans are frozen, bring a saucepan of water to a boil and add the beans. Cook for 3 minutes before draining and running under cold water for 60 seconds to keep their colour (you can also put the drained beans into a bowl of iced water, if easier).
3. If the broccoli is uneven is size, just use a knife to split the bigger pieces down the middle of the stem so they all cook evenly. Put your broccoli into a roasting tray and drizzle with the olive oil, then sprinkle with sea salt. Roast in the oven for 8 minutes. If you are using pumpkin seeds or flaked almonds, chuck them into the broccoli tray to get them nice and toasty!
4. Load your serving bowl with the rocket and sprinkle over the edamame beans. Dress with 2 tablespoons of Apple Cider Vinaigrette and toss well. Note: to avoid overdressing, I'd recommend doing this 1 tablespoon at a time, tossing and testing before adding the next.
5. Chop your goat's cheese into bite-sized pieces and sprinkle over the salad.
6. Cut the avocado into slices or chunks and add to the mix.
7. Add the roasted broccoli, along with your Toasted Furikake Seeds and Paprika Almonds or toasted pumpkin seeds and flaked almonds, saving a few of each to sprinkle for garnish. Toss everything together well, then serve with a final 2–3 tablespoons of Apple Cider Vinaigrette and a finishing sprinkle of almonds and seeds.

100g edamame beans (fresh or frozen)

150g Tenderstem broccoli

2 tsp extra virgin olive oil

2 handfuls of rocket

150g goat's cheese

1 ripe avocado

Sea salt

READY TO ROCK:

3 tbsp Toasted Furikake Seeds (see page 25) or pumpkin seeds

3 tbsp Sweet + Smoky Paprika Almonds (see page 25) or flaked almonds

4–5 tbsp Apple Cider Vinaigrette (see page 76)

TIP:

Add some prawns, salmon or chicken for a protein boost. Boost your batteries with a portion of quinoa or red rice for some extra slow-releasing energy.

ZINGY

Pomegranate + Lime Vinaigrette

Dresses 4–6 salads

Tangy and sweet with subtle twangs of spice, this is the chic big sister to a balsamic vinaigrette. Made from concentrated pomegranate juices, the fruit's molasses is highly nutritious, amping up the benefits of pomegranate itself into a beautiful sweet-and-sour elixir. Pomegranate has been traditionally used to treat chronic diseases and digestive issues, thanks to its density of vitamins and minerals. Fortunately for all of us, it's easier than ever to pick up a bottle of pomegranate molasses – supermarkets and speciality food shops increasingly stock it. An excellent, light dressing that can be used to brighten up so many salads. Don't stop at the recipes here!

½ tsp cumin seeds
½ tsp coriander seeds
2 tbsp pomegranate molasses
40ml red wine vinegar
1 lime (zest and juice)
1 tsp soft light brown sugar
1 tsp Dijon mustard
100ml extra virgin olive oil
2 tsp sea salt

1. Place your cumin and coriander seeds into a small dry frying pan over a medium heat. Swirl gently and allow to toast (careful they don't burn) for 2–3 minutes. You should be able to clearly smell the toasted spices. Allow to cool.
2. Meanwhile, add all the remaining ingredients to a blender. Once cooled, add your toasted seeds. Use the pulse setting to blitz the dressing – you want the liquid to emulsify, but you don't want to over-grind the spices. Rather, aim to crack them so they release their best flavours and give a nice crunch to the dressing. Store in an airtight jar or container in the fridge for up to 1 week.

TRY IT WITH:

+ Sumac Salmon with Honey Carrots, Roasted Tenderstem + Lemony Grains (see page 69)
+ Green + Crunch (see page 80)

The Market Bowl

With Pomegranate + Lime Vinaigrette

Serves 2

+ Long-Build

I still remember the day we decided to remove The Market Bowl from The Salad Project menu. It was a crowd favourite ... and the crowds kicked off. But here she is, back especially for this book. Enjoy a taste of The Salad Project 1.0 in a wholesome and hearty grain bowl, packed with every colour of the rainbow, roasted veggies, crisp apple and salty-sweet Maple Walnuts, all topped with our tangy Pomegranate + Lime Vinaigrette.

1. Preheat the oven to 220°C/200°C fan.
2. Place the rice, water and cooking salt into a medium saucepan over a medium–high heat and bring to a boil. Once boiling, reduce the heat and leave the rice to cook for 25 minutes until soft and chewy.
3. Meanwhile, in a bowl, combine the honey, mustard, balsamic vinegar and garlic granules with a large pinch of sea salt and a good grind of black pepper. Add the chicken thighs and use your hands to ensure the flesh and skin are well coated. Set aside at room temperature.
4. Chop the sweet potato into 5–7cm chunks, leaving the skin on, and place on a large roasting tray. Slice the onion in half through the root, then peel off the papery skin. Remove the root and halve each piece again. Add to the roasting tray. Drizzle 1½ tablespoons of olive oil over the tray, then sprinkle with a generous pinch of sea salt and the dried rosemary. Use your hands to toss the vegetables in the oil and herbs.
5. Add the chicken thighs, skin side up, to the middle of the vegetable tray and place into the oven for 15 minutes until the vegetables are soft and coloured. Pour any remaining marinade from the bowl over the chicken and return to the oven for another 5 minutes to caramelise.
6. While the chicken and vegetables are cooking, dress the kale with 1 tablespoon of olive oil and a pinch of salt, and massage to soften the leaves. Tip onto a serving plate or bowl.
7. Peel the beetroot, then continue using the peeler to create thin rounds or ribbons of beetroot. Dress with the juice of half the lemon, a pinch of caster sugar and a pinch of sea salt. Allow to sit and release its juices.
8. Chop the apple into pieces of a similar size to the sweet potato and dress with the juice of the other half of the lemon to avoid browning.
9. Once the rice is cooked, toss in 2 tablespoons of Pomegranate + Lime Vinaigrette, then mix through the kale. Layer on your roasted vegetables and apple.
10. Slice the chicken thighs and arrange them over the vegetables. Drain the beetroot ribbons of any released liquid, then dot around the salad.
11. Slice the goat's cheese and scatter over the chicken, then dress everything with 4 tablespoons of Pomegranate + Lime Vinaigrette. Finish with a generous sprinkling of Maple Walnuts and a drizzle of olive oil.

200g Camargue red rice

500ml water

¼ tsp fine cooking salt

1 tbsp runny honey

1 tbsp wholegrain mustard

½ tsp balsamic vinegar

½ tsp garlic granules

3–4 boneless chicken thighs, skin on

1 sweet potato

1 red onion

2½ tbsp extra virgin olive oil, plus extra for drizzling

½ tsp dried rosemary

Handful of kale, destemmed, rinsed and dried

1 small raw beetroot

1 lemon (juice)

Pinch of caster sugar

1 apple (Braeburn or similar)

150g goat's cheese

Sea salt and black pepper

READY TO ROCK:

6 tbsp Pomegranate + Lime Vinaigrette (see page 82)

4–5 tbsp Maple Walnuts (see page 24)

TIP:

For a vegetarian alternative, roast some maple + thyme mushrooms (see the tip on page 120) to replace the chicken.

ZINGY

Hot Honey Halloumi + Dill Fattoush
With Pomegranate + Lime Vinaigrette

Serves 2

+ Quick-Build

This delicious fattoush (a traditional Lebanese salad made with fried pitta bread) is piled high with fresh herbs and has a bright acidity that meets its match in the oozingly sweet and salty halloumi. We like chopping the vegetables nice and fine and spooning this from a bowl, using the halloumi like little sticky boats – but this also makes for a gorgeous display salad if you're cooking for a crowd. Just promise you'll cook the halloumi at the last minute; then serve it up straight away.

1. Preheat your oven to 220˚C/200˚C fan.
2. Slice your pittas along the seams to give you 4 ovals, then slice 4 times across the width and 3 times down the length to give you rectangles. Place your pitta chips into a bowl and add the sesame oil, the fennel, cumin and coriander seeds and a pinch of sea salt. Use your hands to mix well and coat your pitta. Place into a roasting dish lined with parchment paper, making sure you use a plastic spatula to scrape all the oil and seeds that haven't stuck to the pitta into the roasting tray too. Roast for 8 minutes, or until golden and crispy. Leave on the tray to cool.
3. Top and tail the radishes, and then cut into quarters. Place into some iced water to crisp up.
4. Slice your cucumber in half lengthways, then use a teaspoon to scrape out the seeds. Slice each half lengthways into thirds, then chop across the strands at 1cm intervals to give you small dice. Place in a serving bowl.
5. Quarter your cherry tomatoes and add them to the bowl.
6. Remove and discard the bottom 5cm of the parsley and dill stems, and pick the mint leaves from the stalks. Set aside a couple of sprigs of dill for garnish, then pile the herbs together and roughly chop before adding to the mixed vegetables. Dress the herby vegetables with 3 tablespoons of Pomegranate + Lime Vinaigrette, then mix in the pitta chips.
7. Slice the halloumi into 1–2cm-thick slices. Heat the olive oil in a frying pan over a medium–high heat. When sizzling hot, add your halloumi in a single layer using metal tongs. After 2 minutes, drizzle 1 tablespoon of Hot Honey over the halloumi, then turn to cook on the other side. Leave for 3 minutes, or until the bottom takes on a dark golden colour. Once it is well coloured, turn over once more to finish colouring the first side. Use tongs to place your warm halloumi over the chopped salad.
8. Top your salad with the radishes and Quick Pickled Onions. Add 3–4 more tablespoons of Pomegranate + Lime Vinaigrette and finish with a generous pinch of sea salt and a couple of sprigs of dill. Serve immediately for the best halloumi texture!

2 pitta breads
1 tbsp toasted sesame oil
½ tsp fennel seeds
½ tsp cumin seeds
½ tsp coriander seeds
120g radishes
1 cucumber
150g cherry tomatoes
15g flat leaf parsley
5g dill
5g mint
225g block of halloumi
2 tbsp extra virgin olive oil
Sea salt

READY TO ROCK:

6–7 tbsp Pomegranate + Lime Vinaigrette (see page 82)
1 tbsp Hot Honey (see page 31)
2 tbsp Quick Pickled Onions (see page 28)

TIP:

Skip the pitta chips and instead warm some whole pittas, line them with a little drizzle of Hot Honey, then fill them with the dressed chopped vegetables and halloumi for something to take on the road.

Lemon + Thyme Vinaigrette

Dresses 4–6 salads

A punchy classic to keep up your sleeve if you need to throw a dressing together pronto. It's also one you can run with to create your own secret flavour weapons: stay close to home by swapping thyme for rosemary; push the boat out a little further by swapping lemon for orange; or really shake things up by swapping in lime, a touch of miso in place of the mustard and some shredded lime leaves instead of thyme. Just make sure you do just that: shake it up, don't blitz.

2 lemons (zest of 1, juice of both), plus extra to taste (optional)

1 garlic clove

1 tbsp wholegrain mustard

1 tsp caster sugar

1 tsp sea salt, plus extra to taste (optional)

10 sprigs of thyme, plus extra to taste (optional)

80ml extra virgin olive oil

Black pepper

1. Grate the zest of 1 lemon into a glass jar. Squeeze in the juice of both lemons.
2. Crush the garlic using the side of your knife or a garlic crusher and a pinch of salt to help grind into a paste. Add to the jar, along with the mustard, sugar, sea salt and a good grind of black pepper.
3. Pick the thyme leaves from the stems and add to the jar, along with the olive oil, then place the lid on the jar and give it a vigorous shake.
4. Taste with a spoon, or by dipping a lettuce leaf in and eating it, and adjust lemon, salt and thyme to taste. Store in an airtight jar or container in the fridge for up to 1 week. Shake vigorously before use.

TRY IT WITH:

+ Green + Crunch (see page 80)
+ The Market Bowl (see page 84)

Garlic + Thyme Chicken, Butter Bean + Sun-Dried Tomato

With Lemon + Thyme Vinaigrette

Serves 2

+ Medium-Build
+ Protein Power

When this recipe was being developed, someone described it as a salad you could eat every day. It's filled with big hitters: juicy chicken breasts, salty tinned anchovies, sun-dried tomatoes and a generous grating of Parmesan. This is a great salad for making use of what might feel like a random assortment of tins and jars kicking about the cupboard, and it couldn't be easier to throw together – particularly if you have some leftover roast chicken you're looking to use up …

1. Preheat the oven to 220°C/200°C fan.
2. In a mixing bowl, mix together the garlic granules, thyme, cooking salt, 3 grinds of black pepper and 2 tablespoons of the olive oil, then add your chicken breasts and coat well. Set aside to marinate while you prepare the remaining ingredients.
3. Drain and rinse your butter beans in a sieve, then tip into a mixing bowl.
4. Roughly chop the sun-dried tomatoes, and add them to the butter bean bowl, followed by the leaves from the sprigs of thyme. Grate in the lemon zest, then add the remaining 2 teaspoons of olive oil and a pinch of sea salt. Mix well.
5. Place your chicken breasts onto a roasting tray and roast in the oven for 20 minutes.
6. Prepare your serving plate with a generous covering of your leaves and basil, and drizzle with 2–3 tablespoons of Lemon + Thyme Vinaigrette. Use your hands to coat the leaves (it's always best to start with less dressing, toss, then add more if needed, than to overdress from the get-go!). Fold your beans and tomato mix through the leaf base until well distributed, then fold in your anchovies.
7. Once the chicken is cooked, let it sit for 5 minutes, then slice it and dress with the juice from half of your lemon. Scatter the chicken over the salad, and dress with 3–4 more tablespoons of Lemon + Thyme Vinaigrette. Finally, use a fine grater or microplane to grate over the Parmesan cheese (generously!) and finish with a couple of basil leaves, a grind of pepper and a drizzle of olive oil.

Ingredients
1 tsp garlic granules
1½ tsp dried thyme
½ tsp fine cooking salt
2 tbsp + 2 tsp extra virgin olive oil, plus extra for drizzling
2 chicken breasts
400g jarred or tinned butter beans
100g sun-dried tomatoes, drained
10 sprigs of thyme
1 lemon (zest of whole, juice of half)
2 large handfuls of mâche or lamb's lettuce, rinsed and dried
Handful of basil leaves, plus extra to garnish
30g tinned anchovies, drained
40g Parmesan
Sea salt and black pepper

READY TO ROCK:

5–7 tbsp Lemon + Thyme Vinaigrette (see page 88)

TIP:

To turn this into a grain bowl that provides a little more bulk, add some red rice and dress it in your vinaigrette before stirring through the salad leaves.

ZINGY

Roasted Courgette + Burrata with Chickpeas + Garlicky Seeds

With Lemon + Thyme Vinaigrette

Serves 2

+ Quick-Build

This salad has been described as 'glamorous', which is what all salads should strive to be. All it takes is the frying up of some courgette slices and the zesting of a lemon, but it serves up a satisfying meal that's suitable for every moment, from a spruced-up Wednesday night in, to a special occasion. It's not all style without substance, though. This salad delivers on complete plant proteins thanks to the combination of lemony chickpeas and garlicky toasted pumpkin seeds. It also delivers on big flavour, for which we owe thanks to our zesty vinaigrette and, lest we forget, the burrata.

1. Slice your courgettes into 2cm rounds. Heat the olive oil in a large frying pan over a medium–high heat. Add your courgette slices in one layer and sprinkle generously with sea salt and black pepper (you may have to do this in batches). Leave the courgettes to caramelise for 5–6 minutes before flipping them to cook on the other side – again, keeping them in one layer.
2. Meanwhile, slice your garlic into 1–2mm slices and set aside.
3. Place the rinsed chickpeas into a small bowl and grate over the zest of your lemon. Add the extra virgin olive oil and a pinch of salt. Mix well and set aside.
4. Once both sides of your courgette slices are nicely browned, take the pan off the heat and add your garlic. Mix it through the courgettes for a couple of minutes. It should cook gently in the residual heat of the pan. Pour the courgettes into a bowl to cool, but don't clean your pan.
5. Add the pumpkin and sunflower seeds to the pan used for the courgettes and place over a low–medium heat. Use a wooden spoon or spatula to mix them through any remaining garlicky oil, and gently toast for 4–5 minutes until the skins of the pumpkin seeds start to split.
6. If using, gently peel the leaves off your radicchio, then rinse and dry them well. Lay the radicchio or bitter salad leaves onto your serving platter, or split across 2 plates. Drizzle with 3 tablespoons of your Lemon + Thyme Vinaigrette. Next, pour over your chickpeas, followed by your courgettes.
7. Drain your burrata from its packet and gently tear over your salad. Finish with 2 more tablespoons of Lemon + Thyme Vinaigrette and top with your toasted seeds.

2 courgettes	
2 tbsp olive oil	
1 large garlic clove	
570g jar chickpeas (preferably the large Spanish ones) or 400g tin, drained and rinsed	
1 lemon (zest)	
1 tbsp extra virgin olive oil	
25g pumpkin seeds	
25g sunflower seeds	
½ radicchio or 80g mixed bitter-leaf salad	
150g burrata	
Sea salt and black pepper	

READY TO ROCK:

5 tbsp Lemon + Thyme Vinaigrette (see page 88)

TIP:

Add some extra colour by mixing in some yellow courgettes or purple aubergine, and some cherry tomatoes, blistered over a high heat in the courgette pan.

ZINGY

Romesco Drizzle Dressing

Dresses 4–6 salads

There was a time when a romesco- or muhammara-style dressing, dip or marinade made an appearance at just about every menu tasting we held through the year. This is something we have been whizzing up at home since the early days of The Salad Project, and was actually one of the inspirations behind this book's concept. It takes literal seconds to make and turns a late-night refuel into something nutritious, colourful and absolutely delicious. Keep this in a jar in your fridge and you can whack it on anything to add not only great flavour, but also extra veggies, healthy fats and antioxidants, instantly.

30g toasted hazelnuts (for untoasted, see step 1)

140g roasted red peppers from a jar, drained

2 tsp white wine vinegar, plus extra to taste (optional)

1 tsp smoked paprika

¼ tsp cayenne pepper, plus extra to taste (optional)

6–7 mint leaves

1 tsp soft light brown sugar

50ml extra virgin olive oil

1 tsp sea salt, plus extra to taste (optional)

1. If your hazelnuts aren't pre-toasted, preheat the oven to 220°C/200°C fan and line a baking tray with parchment paper.
2. Put the hazelnuts onto the tray (it's easiest to do this in a big batch and store the extra hazelnuts in a jar for later – they are great chopped on top of any salad!). Roast for 5 minutes, then remove the tray from the oven and place the hazelnuts onto a clean tea towel. Allow to cool for a minute. Fold the tea towel over the nuts and rub to loosen and remove the skins. Don't worry if they aren't completely removed – they are just getting blended up (and add nice colour to a salad when used whole/chopped).
3. Place the toasted hazelnuts and all other ingredients into a blender and pulse to keep chunky, or blitz until smooth.
4. Taste – add more sea salt or white wine vinegar if needed. You can also ramp up the cayenne if you'd like a spicier dressing! Store in an airtight jar or container in the fridge for up to 1 week.

TRY IT WITH:

+ Green 'n' Minty Whole Grain Pasta Salad (see page 143)
+ Crispy New Potatoes, Whipped Ricotta + Pickled Radish (see page 133)
+ Harissa Steak + Giant Couscous with Pickled Onions + Pistachios (see page 70)

Spiced Cauliflower with Smoky Toasted Almonds + Hot Honey Labneh

With Romesco Drizzle Dressing

Serves 2
+ Long-Build

ZINGY

Cauliflower and romesco really are a killer combination, and here they're served up on a light, herby salad with a creamy base of labneh, which cuts through the zing of the red pepper drizzle and delivers a great protein hit. This is a perfect midweek meal or weekend lunch when you're looking for something that won't weigh you down, but will keep you feeling full and energised until your next meal. Labneh can be ready within 20 minutes, so don't be put off; but for the creamiest texture, you can start dripping your yoghurt a day in advance.

1. Preheat the oven to 220°C/200°C fan.
2. Line a sieve with a clean muslin cloth and place the sieve over a bowl. Dollop the yoghurt into the muslin and lift the corners to pull the yoghurt into a ball, tying the excess material with an elastic band. Leave it to sit at room temperature in the sieve, to allow the whey from the yoghurt to drip into the bowl underneath. The longer you leave this to drip, the thicker the labneh will be, so do it the day before if you have time. If not, don't panic – it will still improve in texture after just 20 minutes.
3. Finely slice your cucumber using a knife or mandolin, and place in a jar or small airtight container. Add the cooking salt, sugar, dill, vinegar and water and leave for 15 minutes to gently pickle.
4. Meanwhile, mix the spices, 1 teaspoon of sea salt and the olive oil into a paste-like marinade in a medium–large mixing bowl. Chop the cauliflower into florets and add to the bowl with the marinade. Use your hands to fully coat the cauliflower – it will feel like there is not enough marinade, but there is! Place the cauliflower onto a roasting tray, scraping out all of the marinade left in the bowl with a plastic spatula. Roast for 20 minutes until golden.
5. Use kitchen paper to roughly clean out the cauliflower bowl, then use the bowl to combine the watercress and most of the parsley. Squeeze in the lemon juice and sprinkle a pinch of salt into the leaves. Toss gently with your hands.
6. Slice the avocado and toss into the leaf mix.
7. Open out the muslin cloth and discard the liquid from the bowl. Dry the bowl with some kitchen paper, then pour the dripped yoghurt into it. Add the rose harissa, honey and 4 pinches of sea salt, and fold through.
8. Dollop the labneh onto the bottom of your serving plate and spread it slightly with a spoon. Pile on your leaf and avocado mix and drizzle with 2 tablespoons of Romesco Drizzle Dressing. Pile on the roasted cauliflower and top with pickled cucumbers and Sweet + Smoky Paprika Almonds. Finish with another 3–4 tablespoons of Romesco Drizzle Dressing, a drizzle of Hot Honey (if using) and the remaining parsley.

250g natural yoghurt

½ cucumber

1 tsp fine cooking salt

1 tsp caster sugar

Small handful of dill, chopped

60ml white wine vinegar

120ml water

1 tsp smoked paprika

1 tsp ground cumin

1 tsp cumin seeds

1 tbsp extra virgin olive oil

½ cauliflower

Large handful of watercress

Large handful of flat leaf parsley

½ lemon (juice)

1 ripe avocado

2 tsp rose harissa

2 tsp runny honey

Sea salt

READY TO ROCK:

5–6 tbsp Romesco Drizzle Dressing (see page 92)

2 tbsp Sweet + Smoky Paprika Almonds (see page 25) or some toasted flaked almonds

1 tbsp Hot Honey (see page 31) or just honey plus a pinch of chilli flakes (optional)

TIP:

For a plant-based labneh, sub out the natural yoghurt for an unsweetened plant-based yoghurt alternative and add the juice of a lemon. It may need a little longer to drip, but follow the same process.

Paprika Chicken Thigh with Nutty Grains + Roasted Peppers

With Romesco Drizzle Dressing

Serves 2

+ Medium-Build
+ Brain + Body Fuel

A wholesome, hearty plate of the good stuff. This is a recipe to make for all occasions, from whipping up a pick-me-up for a mate or refuelling after an evening run, to impressing a date. It's full of flavour – I love using herbs as salad leaves in their own right, as we've done with the parsley here – and it's gorgeously vibrant, with a colour profile I'm partial to given my name. This is a great recipe to use with cauliflower roasted in the same spices if you're plant-based or just doubling up on veg.

1. Take a medium-sized mixing bowl and combine the garlic granules, spices, sugar, 2 tablespoons of the olive oil and ½ teaspoon of sea salt into a paste. Add your chicken thighs to the bowl and, using your hands or some tongs, turn the chicken so each piece is well coated across every surface. Set aside to marinate.
2. Cook the bulgur wheat or freekeh with the stock jelly or cube according to packet instructions. Drain once cooked.
3. Heat 1 tablespoon of the olive oil in a large frying pan over a medium–high heat. Using metal tongs, add the marinated chicken thighs and press into the pan to ensure as much of the surface of the meat as possible can caramelise. Leave to cook on one side for 6 minutes until well coloured, before flipping over to cook on the other side for a further 6 minutes. Once done, remove the cooked chicken from the heat and let sit for a couple of minutes before slicing.
4. While the chicken cooks, remove any remaining seeds from the roasted peppers and slice into 5cm-wide rings or slices.
5. Roughly chop the dill and a small handful of the parsley, discarding the stems, then dress the cooked grains with the remaining 1 tablespoon of olive oil, the chopped herbs and a pinch of sea salt.
6. To assemble the salad, cover your serving plate with the rocket and remaining parsley (use the whole herb for this bit!). Top with your cooked grains and drizzle with 3 tablespoons of Romesco Drizzle Dressing. Next, lay on your roasted peppers and 2 tablespoons of the pomegranate seeds.
7. Slice the chicken (or leave it whole, if you'd prefer) and scatter over the salad. Dress with 3 more tablespoons of Romesco Drizzle Dressing, followed by the Sweet + Smoky Paprika Almonds and a final tablespoon of pomegranate seeds.

Ingredients
1 tsp garlic granules
1 tsp paprika
¼ tsp cayenne pepper
½ tsp caster sugar
4 tbsp extra virgin olive oil
3–4 chicken thighs, skinless and boneless
150g coarse bulgur wheat or freekeh
½ vegetable stock jelly or ½ cube
2 roasted red peppers from a jar, drained
Small handful of dill
Large handful of flat leaf parsley
2 handfuls of rocket
3 tbsp pomegranate seeds
Sea salt

READY TO ROCK:

6 tbsp Romesco Drizzle Dressing (see page 92)

3 tbsp Sweet + Smoky Paprika Almonds (see page 25) or toasted flaked almonds

TIP:

For an extra flavour hit, use skin-on chicken thighs and cook skin side down until nice and crispy, before flipping over to finish cooking the meat.

Preserved Lemon + Sour Cream Dressing

Dresses 4–6 salads

This dressing was the result of an accident that came out of a bit of play time in the test kitchen during a shoot. I was completely silenced when I took a spoonful on camera and decided, in that moment, that this was the best dressing I had ever tasted. If you're looking for mouth-dribblingly delicious zing, this is she – and she's your new go-to for dressing a green salad, roast chicken or potato salad, or for mopping up with pitta bread and ice-cold radishes.

1. Chop your preserved lemons into small pieces and remove any pips that pop out in the process. Place your chopped lemons and their liquid into a high-speed blender, along with the other ingredients. Blend until silky smooth.
2. You can have a play with the amount of parsley you want to add – either omitting it entirely if you'd like a pale cream dressing, or cranking up the quantity for a brighter green colour. Store in an airtight jar or container in the fridge for up to 1 week.

2 preserved lemons, plus 4 tbsp of their brine

100g mayonnaise

100g sour cream or crème fraîche (if you're plant-based, sub the mayonnaise and sour cream for 200g vegan mayonnaise)

20g Worcestershire sauce (if you're plant-based, skip this or switch for 10g balsamic vinegar)

1 lemon (zest and juice)

10g flat leaf parsley

A few grinds of black pepper

TRY IT WITH:

+ Miso Chicken with Crispy Spiced Chickpeas + Pickled Cucumbers (see page 48)
+ Sumac Salmon with Honey Carrots, Roasted Tenderstem + Lemony Grains (see page 69)
+ Roasted Courgette + Burrata with Chickpeas + Garlicky Seeds (see page 90)
+ Harissa Steak + Giant Couscous with Pickled Onions + Pistachios (see page 70)

Crispy Spiced Lamb, Aubergine + Freekeh with Pickled Onions

With Preserved Lemon + Sour Cream Dressing

Serves 2

+ Medium-Build

Lamb is the perfect pairing for this mouth-wateringly zingy dressing, as its fattiness and the deep, spiced, caramelised flavours that come from crisping it up on the hob cut through the acid and get your taste buds really firing, particularly thanks to our epic mix of toasted seeds (all of which contribute to your daily plants, FYI). There's nothing more satisfying than meat not being allowed to steal all the attention from a dish, and in this recipe our Preserved Lemon + Sour Cream Dressing really stands her ground against some punchy lamb.

1. Preheat the oven to 220°C/200°C fan and line a small roasting tray with parchment paper.
2. Cut your aubergine into roughly 5cm cubes and place into a bowl. Add 1 tablespoon of the olive oil, a pinch of sea salt and a few grinds of pepper. Mix well with your hands. Pour onto your lined roasting tray and place in the oven for 20 minutes.
3. Heat 1 teaspoon of the olive oil in a medium frying pan over a medium–high heat. Add your spices and move around the pan to keep the seeds moving while they toast to avoid burning. Once you can smell the aromatics of the spices releasing – around 2–3 minutes – add your lamb mince and break it up with a wooden spoon. Avoid 'mashing' the lamb, and instead tease it apart to keep the mince strands intact. Once broken down, mix well to distribute the spices. Add ½ teaspoon sea salt and mix well through the lamb. Keep the lamb cooking over a medium–high heat, stirring every few minutes to avoid the lamb burning or sticking to the pan, until dark brown and crispy. This should take around 25 minutes. Trust us, this can get really nice and crispy, so keep going!
4. While your lamb is crisping up, cook the grains with the stock jelly or cube according to the packet instructions. Drain when ready.
5. Take your salad platter or a couple of plates and cover them with the mâche or lamb's lettuce.
6. Slice your radicchio into strands, if using, and mix into your green leaves. Alternatively, mix the bitter-leaf mix with the green leaves.
7. Stir the chopped flat leaf parsley through your cooked grains, then pour over your leaf base. Next add your roasted aubergine, then drizzle 3 tablespoons of Preserved Lemon + Sour Cream dressing over the top. Sprinkle over your crispy lamb and its whole spices. Top with a couple of pinches of Quick Pickled Onions, and dress with 3 tablespoons more of the Preserved Lemon + Sour Cream Dressing.

---

1 aubergine

1 tbsp + 1 tsp extra virgin olive oil

½ tsp cumin seeds

½ tsp fennel seeds

½ tsp coriander seeds

½ tsp ground cinnamon

½ tsp ground cumin

¼ tsp ground chilli powder

250g lamb mince (20% fat)

150g bulgur wheat or freekeh

½ vegetable stock jelly or ½ cube

30g mâche or lamb's lettuce, rinsed and dried

½ radicchio or 60g salad leaf mix containing purple/bitter leaves

Handful of flat leaf parsley, roughly chopped

Sea salt and black pepper

READY TO ROCK:

6 tbsp Preserved Lemon + Sour Cream Dressing (see page 98)

2 tbsp Quick Pickled Onions (see page 28)

TIP:

Mop up this salad with some warm pitta or flatbreads.

Tamari Tofu with Vermicelli Noodles, Cabbage Slaw + Crispy Onions

With Preserved Lemon + Sour Cream Dressing

Serves 2

+ Medium-Build
+ Protein Power

We love experimenting with fusing different cuisines, and this is the kooky result of one of those experiments. Here we have a Middle Eastern(ish) dressing bringing citrusy, salty life to some noodles and a sweet miso tofu, serving up a reminder that salads don't need to have rules, or leafy bases.

1. In a wide-based bowl, mix together the maple syrup, tamari, 1 tablespoon of the sesame oil and the miso paste until well combined. Chop the tofu into 2.5cm cubes and place into the marinade, turning each piece to ensure it's coated on all sides.
2. Finely shred the red cabbage, using a knife, mandolin or vegetable peeler, and place on the base of a serving plate.
3. Pick the leaves from the parsley and use your hands to distribute it through the cabbage base.
4. Slice your spring onion and sprinkle through the cabbage. Dress your base with 3 tablespoons of Preserved Lemon + Sour Cream Dressing.
5. Cook the vermicelli noodles according to the packet instructions, then drain in a sieve and run under cold water to cool and avoid sticking. After rinsing, dress with the lemon juice and a pinch of sea salt, and use tongs to place the noodles over the cabbage on the serving plate.
6. Heat 2 teaspoons of the sesame oil in a frying pan over a high heat. Use tongs to place the marinated tofu into the hot oil and fry on each side for 3–4 minutes until golden and crisp. When all sides are well coloured, add any remaining marinade to the pan and reduce the heat to medium-high while the marinade thickens and caramelises around the tofu. Add the sesame seeds to the pan and toss to coat the tofu.
7. Arrange the tofu over the noodles and finish with another 3 tablespoons of Preserved Lemon + Sour Cream Dressing and the Crispy Onions.

Ingredients
2 tbsp maple syrup
2 tbsp tamari
1 tbsp + 2 tsp toasted sesame oil
1 tsp white miso paste
250g super-firm tofu
⅓ red cabbage
Large handful of flat leaf parsley
1 spring onion
250g vermicelli noodles
½ lemon (juice)
3 tbsp sesame seeds
Sea salt

READY TO ROCK:

6 tbsp Preserved Lemon + Sour Cream Dressing (see page 98)

4 tbsp Crispy Onions (see page 24 for home-made, or shop-bought works fine)

TIP:

Use the dressing as a sauce for the noodles and top with tofu, salmon or steak for a super-speedy, low-faff dinner.

Ballymaloe's French Dressing

Dresses 8–10 salads

Before joining The Salad Project, I studied at Ballymaloe Cookery School in Ireland. It taught me three key lessons about salad: 1) how to identify every type of lettuce leaf in the space of ten minutes; 2) that the best salads combine quality ingredients, colour and contrasting textures; 3) that you should always eat green salads with your hands. While it might not fly to tell our Salad Project customers to eat our salads with their fingers, I wanted to pay homage to the place that instilled my love of stunning veg – where I was revising for exams in lettuce leaves. Here's a classic French dressing, called the Ballymaloe Cookery School Dressing, designed by Darina Allen. We've doubled the quantities, because you can never have too much of this in your fridge.

2 garlic cloves

2 tsp runny honey (preferably Irish)

1 tsp Dijon mustard or English mustard powder

4 tbsp white wine vinegar, plus extra to taste (optional)

250ml extra virgin olive oil

½ tsp sea salt, plus extra to taste (optional)

Good grind of black pepper, plus extra to taste (optional)

1. Peel and crush your garlic using the side of a knife or a garlic crusher and a little sea salt to help turn it into a smooth paste.
2. Place all ingredients into a jam jar and screw the lid on tight. Give the jar a good shake to bring all the ingredients together.
3. Taste by dipping a lettuce leaf or teaspoon into the dressing to see how intense the flavour is. Adjust the salt, pepper and vinegar to taste. Store in an airtight jar or container in the fridge for up to 1 week. Shake vigorously before use.

TRY IT WITH:

+ Green + Crunch (see page 80)
+ Roasted Courgette + Burrata Salad with Chickpeas + Garlicky Seeds (see page 90)

ZINGY

Tuna Steak Niçoise + Jammy Eggs
With Ballymaloe's French Dressing

Serves 2

+ Medium-Build
+ Brain + Body Fuel

Salade Niçoise is iconic for good reason. But heavy is the head that wears the crown – there is a lot of controversy surrounding what can really be deemed a true Niçoise. We're not claiming to be the experts, but instead have put The Salad Project twist on this classic to give you a big, bold and beautiful salad that won't leave you hungry. New potatoes are a great source of vitamin C, and their skins are loaded with fibre, which aids digestion, so don't let the best bit go to waste.

300g baby or new potatoes	
2 tbsp + 2 tsp extra virgin olive oil	
1 tbsp fine cooking salt	
3–4 eggs	
100g green beans	
1 cos lettuce	
10 cherry tomatoes	
2 tuna steaks	
2 tbsp capers, drained	
Sea salt and black pepper	

READY TO ROCK:

5–6 tbsp Ballymaloe's French Dressing (see page 104)

1. Preheat your oven to 220°C/200°C fan.
2. Rinse and scrub your potatoes. Leave the smallest potatoes whole and chop any larger ones into bite-sized halves or quarters. Place into a large mixing bowl. Add 2 tablespoons of the olive oil, 2 generous pinches of sea salt and roughly 10 grinds of black pepper. Mix well until the potatoes are well coated, then pour into a roasting tray. Roast for 25 minutes, giving them a stir or shake every 10 minutes to avoid them sticking to the pan.
3. Bring a large pot of water to a boil over a medium–high heat and add the fine cooking salt. Carefully add your eggs and cook for 6½ minutes.
4. Place the green beans into a sieve and sit on top of the egg-boiling pan. Cover with a lid and let the beans steam for 3 minutes, then remove the sieve and rinse the beans under cold water. Set aside.
5. Place an empty bowl under the tap. Once your eggs are cooked, carefully place into the bowl and run the cold water tap for 3–4 minutes until the eggs stop cooking in their residual heat. If you simply sit the eggs in static cold water, the eggs will heat the water, so keep the tap running! Alternatively, place them in an ice bath.
6. Remove any gnarly outer leaves from the cos lettuce, then chop off the bottom and cut diagonally down the length of the cos to give you 5–7cm pieces. Spread over a large serving dish and dress with 2 tablespoons of Ballymaloe's French Dressing.
7. Halve the cherry tomatoes and lay your tomatoes, steamed beans and roasted crispy potatoes over the lettuce.
8. Rub 1 teaspoon of olive oil, a pinch of salt and a couple of grinds of pepper into each of the tuna steaks. Heat a frying pan over a high heat and, when hot, add your tuna. Cook for 45 seconds on each side, using tongs to flip, so that the outsides of the fish are seared but the inside stays nice and rare (reduce this to 30 seconds if the steaks are quite thin, or cook for longer if you prefer well-cooked tuna). Leave to sit for a couple of minutes.
9. While the tuna is resting, peel your eggs and slice into halves. Season each with a little sea salt and black pepper.
10. Slice the tuna against the grain of the fish, and season with a pinch of sea salt. Place the eggs and tuna slices over the salad and scatter with the capers. Finish with 3–4 tablespoons of Ballymaloe's French Dressing.

TIP:

While you're at it, boil up some extra jammy eggs and keep them in the fridge for 1 week – they're a great way to turn some leftovers into a proper meal.

A Spoonful of Goodness

With Ballymaloe's French Dressing

Serves 2

+ **Medium-Build**
+ **Protein Power**

There's something incredibly satisfying about eating a salad with a spoon, and even more so when you're shovelling in pure goodness. This salad is loaded with health benefits, including plant-based protein in the quinoa base and heart-healthy fats in the avocado and olive oil. It's also packed with polyphenols with antioxidant and anti-inflammatory properties, and there are vitamins in the avocado, citrus, sugar snaps, herbs and cucumber that work to help protect your skin from oxidative damage. So, see this fresh, citrusy and satisfying salad as a super-strong base on which to build and customise with different protein options, or as a salad worthy of a good spooning in and of itself.

1. Add the quinoa to a medium saucepan with the water. Add the fine cooking salt and stir. Bring to a boil over a high heat, then reduce the heat to medium–high and allow to bubble gently for 20–25 minutes until the water is absorbed and the quinoa is soft and fluffy.
2. While the quinoa is cooking, slice each sugar snap pea into 4 pieces at an angle and place into a large mixing bowl.
3. Slice the cucumber in half lengthways, and use a teaspoon to scoop out the seeds. Dice the remaining cucumber into roughly 2cm pieces and add to the sugar snap peas.
4. Pick the herb leaves from their stems and roughly chop the leaves all together. Add them to the vegetable bowl, reserving a few for garnish.
5. Once your quinoa is cooked, pour it into a clean bowl and add the olive oil, and lemon zest and juice. Mix through with a fork to fluff it up. Place the quinoa in the fridge for 10 minutes to allow it to cool slightly, then add it to the green vegetables, along with 3 tablespoons of Ballymaloe's French Dressing, the chilli flakes, if using, and the Toasted Furikake Seeds. Mix well.
6. Chop the avocado into chunky pieces and fold through the mix. Pour onto a serving plate.
7. Crumble over the feta, if using, then slice the spring onion from root to tip and scatter over the top.
8. Dress with another 2 tablespoons of Ballymaloe's French Dressing and finish with the reserved chopped herbs.

200g mixed-colour quinoa

700ml water

½ tsp fine cooking salt

60g sugar snap peas

½ cucumber

Handful of basil

Handful of mint

Handful of flat leaf parsley

1 tbsp extra virgin olive oil

½ lemon (zest and juice)

1 tbsp chilli flakes (optional)

1 ripe avocado

75g feta (optional)

1 spring onion

READY TO ROCK:

5 tbsp Ballymaloe French Dressing (see page 104)

4 tbsp Toasted Furikake Seeds (see page 25) or toasted pumpkin seeds

TIP:

This is a great dish to have to hand in the fridge as a way of boosting the nutrient density of any post-work meal. Double the volumes above and keep some in the fridge to bulk up any other recipes in this book.

Brown Butter + Miso Vinaigrette

Dresses 4–6 salads

There are few better smells in this world than browning butter, and this dressing captures that smell (and all its nutty deliciousness …) in a vinaigrette. A great umami dressing with a deep brown butter flavour cut through with ever-so-slightly sweet balsamic and salty miso, it's best used warm as a drizzle over salads, roasted veggies or a bowl of pasta. This recipe is a great way of pushing the boat out if you're well and truly wedded to the vinaigrette life. An efficient way of adding complex flavours, simply.

170g unsalted butter
3 tbsp good-quality balsamic vinegar
3 tbsp red wine vinegar
1 tsp white miso paste
Sea salt

1. Place your butter in a sturdy saucepan with edges high enough to ensure it doesn't spit or foam over while browning. Let the butter melt over a medium heat, swirling the pan to ensure it cooks evenly as it melts entirely. As it starts to brown, it will start foaming – keep swirling the pan to allow you to see the colour of the butter, and use your nose to judge when it's reached the point of browning. The colour should be toasty brown, and the smell should be deep, warm and nutty. Remove your butter from the heat and, taking a heat-proof bowl, pour the liquid through a metal sieve to catch the brown buttermilk solids. Discard the solids and allow the melted butter to cool.
2. Meanwhile, take a jar and, using a whisk, mix together your balsamic and red wine vinegars and your miso. Whisk until smooth.
3. Once your melted butter has cooled, add to the vinegar blend and whisk well with a fork, or put the lid on the jar and shake vigorously.
4. Use a teaspoon, or dip in a spare salad leaf, to taste – depending on the miso brand you're using, it will probably need salt. Add a generous pinch if so, then shake again. Repeat until you're happy with the flavour of your dressing. Store in an airtight jar or container in the fridge for up to 1 week. **Note:** this will solidify in the fridge, so gently warm it by popping your jar in a pan of hot water. Alternatively, spoon it directly into a small pan to warm through, or microwave for 10 seconds for a thicker drizzle, and 20 seconds for a classic vinaigrette.

TRY IT WITH:

+ Peaches + Cream (see page 144)
+ Paprika Chicken Thigh with Nutty Grains + Roasted Peppers (see page 96)
+ The Market Bowl (see page 84)

The Octoberfeast: Maple Chicken + Chorizo Grain Bowl

with Brown Butter + Miso Vinaigrette

Serves 2

+ Long-Build

ZINGY

Sage and miso are a match made in heaven. Combine that with sweet maple syrup and a nutty brown butter vinaigrette, and you have the perfect autumnal salad. Hence why we called it the 'Octoberfeast' when it launched as a seasonal special. But while it will certainly suffice as a meal for two, don't let the name fool you into thinking this is a heavy dish – the apple cider slaw, fresh apple and Quick Pickled Onions keep this salad fresh and zingy.

1. Preheat your oven to 210°C/190°C fan and line a roasting tray with parchment paper.
2. In a bowl, add 2 teaspoons of olive oil and a pinch of sea salt to your kale and use your hands to massage it in. Set aside on a serving plate to relax.
3. Take your chorizo and carefully use your knife to remove the thin skin coating it – this can make your chorizo tough and chewy once cooked. Now slice your chorizo into 1cm-thick coins. In a medium-sized mixing bowl, combine 2 tablespoons of olive oil with the maple syrup, wholegrain mustard, shredded sage, 1 tablespoon of Brown Butter + Miso Vinaigrette and a pinch of sea salt. Mix well. Add your chicken thighs and chorizo and coat with the marinade – it's easiest to use your hands here to ensure it's all well coated. Place onto the lined tray and roast in the oven. After 10 minutes, give the meat a little baste (i.e. spoon any juices back over it so it caramelises nicely). Return to the oven for another 15 minutes.
4. Meanwhile, weigh the giant couscous into a saucepan and add the vegetable stock jelly or cube and water. Bring to a boil over a high heat, then reduce the heat to medium to simmer the couscous for 6 minutes, or until cooked through. Pour into a sieve to drain, then rinse with cold water to avoid sticking. Place in a bowl and add 2 tablespoons of Brown Butter + Miso Vinaigrette. Mix through with a fork and spoon over your kale on a serving plate.
5. Using a knife, mandolin or vegetable peeler, shred your cabbage into a small bowl. Dress with the apple cider vinegar and a pinch of sea salt, mixing with your hands. Let it sit for a few minutes to soften.
6. Chop your apple into small cubes and add to your cabbage, then scatter both over your kale and couscous.
7. Slice your chicken and add this and the chorizo to the serving plate – be sure to drizzle any marinade from the tray over the chicken at this point.
8. Finish your salad with a scattering of Quick Pickled Onions and Maple Walnuts, then dress generously with 4 tablespoons of Brown Butter + Miso Vinaigrette. Either toss to mix up all the flavours, or build each ingredient around the plate, if that's more your style.

2 tbsp + 2 tsp extra virgin olive oil
Large handful of kale, destemmed, rinsed, dried and chopped
20cm piece of chorizo
1½ tbsp maple syrup
1½ tsp wholegrain mustard
4 sage leaves, shredded
3–4 chicken thighs, skinless and boneless
150g giant couscous
1 vegetable stock jelly or 1 cube
500ml water
¼ red cabbage
2 tsp apple cider vinegar
1 apple (Braeburn or similar)
Sea salt

READY TO ROCK:

7 tbsp Brown Butter + Miso Vinaigrette (see page 110)
2 tbsp Quick Pickled Onions (see page 28)
2 tbsp Maple Walnuts (see page 24)

TIP:

Warm the Brown Butter + Miso Vinaigrette in the microwave or by placing the jar in a pan of hot water before dressing this salad.

Roasted Squash, Stracciatella + Toasted Maple Buckwheat

with Brown Butter + Miso Vinaigrette

Serves 2

+ Long-Build

ZINGY

This recipe is autumn salad-ified, but swap out the squash for some roasted peaches and you've got the perfect summer salad. If you have your dressing ready to shake and your buckwheat already toasted, you can throw this one together so easily with just one baking tray, a small mixing bowl and a plate.

1. Preheat the oven to 200°C/180°C fan.
2. Gently heat a dry frying pan over a medium heat, then add the green buckwheat groats, the olive oil, a pinch of sea salt and the smoked paprika. Stir to coat the buckwheat, then continue stirring regularly for 3–4 minutes until the groats have turned a deep golden. Set aside to cool.
3. Chop the squash in half and place each half skin side up on a baking tray. Drizzle with olive oil and season with a good pinch of sea salt. Roast for 30 minutes, until a knife slides through the skin without resistance and the skin is blistering.
4. Meanwhile, pop your rocket into a mixing bowl. Add the lemon zest and juice. Use your fingers to gently toss the rocket in the zest and juice. Pile onto a serving plate or low-sided bowl.
5. Place your burrata on top of the rocket and gently tear open to release its stracciatella (curds).
6. When your squash is ready, remove from the oven and cut into crescents, keeping the skin intact. Dot around and on top of your stracciatella.
7. Heat the butter in the frying pan and, when bubbling, add the sage leaves and coat to fry. Baste for 2 minutes until crisp, then remove from the pan. Drain the sage leaves on some kitchen towel, then sprinkle over your squash.
8. Finally, scatter the toasted buckwheat over your salad and drizzle generously with your Brown Butter + Miso Vinaigrette. Finish with a pinch of sea salt and a sprinkling of pink peppercorns, if using.

80g green buckwheat groats (see tip on page 65)
1 tbsp extra virgin olive oil, plus extra for drizzling
Pinch of smoked paprika
1 Delica squash or ½ butternut squash, seeds removed
Large handful of rocket, rinsed and dried
½ lemon (zest and juice)
150g burrata
2 tbsp salted butter
8 sage leaves
Pinch of pink peppercorns (optional)
Sea salt

READY TO ROCK:

6 tbsp Brown Butter + Miso Vinaigrette (see page 110)

TIP:

If you want to swap out squash for roasted peaches, halve or quarter your peaches and remove the stones. Place them on a parchment-lined baking tray and drizzle with olive oil and a couple of splashes of balsamic vinegar. Sprinkle with sea salt. Roast for 10 minutes until soft but still holding their shape. Best served warm!

Herby
114–151

Unsurprisingly, at The Salad Project we love green on green, so we are big fans of herby dressings. Using herbs to whip up flavourful and fresh dressings could not be simpler, and not only do herby dressings add a whole extra layer of plants to any salad, but they are also bright and beautiful in colour, making anything they dress hard to resist.

Herbs can be used in dressings of all styles – creamy, zingy and spicy – but they deserve their own category because there are so many ways to play with them, and even more ways to make the most of what they have to offer.

KEY CHARACTERISTIC:

Goodness-giving and gorgeously green

BEST WHEN:

Left chunky or blended smooth – the choice is yours

BUILD YOUR OWN

Curate your own creamy combinations with this simple formula:

(SALT) (ACID) (FAT) (SWEET)

The most important elements in a herby dressing are – shock – the herbs. So, when getting creative, stick to our classic formula and experiment with adding all things green, seeing how the vibe changes depending on what you choose to play with from our four key categories. Here are some good herbs for getting creative with:

- Chives
- Dill
- Flat leaf parsley
- Fresh coriander
- Mint
- Basil
- Thai basil
- Lovage
- Sorrel
- Tarragon

DOS AND DON'TS FOR HERBY DRESSINGS:

+ Herby dressings can be silky smooth or left chunky – experiment with different textures to find your favourite.
+ Herby dressings will start to discolour if exposed to oxygen, so keep them sealed and just give them a good stir before using – the darker colour doesn't mean they aren't safe to use, but their flavour may be a bit muted.
+ Don't be afraid to use herby dressings as an excuse to use up wilting herbs (or salad leaves) – they are a great way to increase herbs' lifespan and avoid waste.
+ Do feel free to swap in your favourite herbs to any of the recipes that follow.
+ Herby dressings are a great way of bringing freshness and colour to carbs – use them to dress potatoes, pastas and grains.

The SP Green Goddess Dressing

Dresses 4–6 salads

We are well aware this is not a 'green goddess' dressing in the true sense of the term (traditionally a creamy, green dressing made from a base of avocado and mayonnaise). Ours is more like a multi-herb, super-fresh pesto, but it is the green dressing that has been bringing our bestselling salad, The GOAT (see opposite), to life since day one of The Salad Project, so, for that reason, we think it's earned its goddess status. If you have tried The GOAT, we're sure you will agree.

1. Chop the bottom 5cm off the basil stems and place the remainder of the basil into a blender.
2. Add all remaining ingredients to the blender and pulse to purée the herbs and liquids. Once it reaches a pesto-like texture, you can stop (which is what we prefer to do), or you can keep blitzing until completely smooth. Store in an airtight jar or container in the fridge for up to 1 week. The herbs and olive oil will separate over time, so just give it a good shake or stir before using.

25g basil
25g mint leaves
25g baby spinach
1 tsp Dijon mustard
1 lemon (juice)
¼ tsp caster sugar
115ml extra virgin olive oil
30ml water
1 tsp sea salt

TRY IT WITH:

+ Burrata + Spring (see page 13)
+ Steak, Sweet Potato + Rocket Salad (see page 138)
+ Tomatoes on Toast with Minty Courgette Ribbons + Capers (see page 66)

The GOAT

With The SP Green Goddess Dressing

Serves 2

+ Medium-Build

HERBY

We didn't know at the time of creating The GOAT that it would, quite literally, live up to its name as the undisputed bestselling salad across our sites, but here we are. And now, here you go. There's something magical about the combination of creamy goat's cheese, a fresh, green, herby dressing, roasted sweet potatoes and, of course, Maple Walnuts. What makes this salad so special is its ability to feel fresh, bright and flavoursome, while throwing some full-flavour curve balls that deliver little moments of sweet, 'mind-blowing' (not our words …) indulgence. In short, it does what all GREAT salads do: The GOAT keeps you guessing.

1. Preheat the oven to 220°C/200°C fan.
2. Measure the brown sugar, sriracha, miso paste, tamari, lime juice and 1 teaspoon of sesame oil into a mixing bowl or plastic container and stir until smooth. Add the chicken thighs and use your hands or tongs to ensure the marinade reaches every crevice of the chicken. Leave to sit for 20–30 minutes.
3. Meanwhile, chop the sweet potato in half down its length and lay the cut sides down on the chopping board. Cut one more time down the length, then, keeping the 2 batons together, slice horizontally into 1cm pieces, so you end up with quarter slices. Place into a roasting tray big enough to fit them in a single layer.
4. Pull the pines of the rosemary sprig to remove from the stem and chop very finely.
5. To the sweet potatoes, add the olive oil, chopped rosemary, garlic granules and sea salt. Use your hands to coat. Place in the oven for 15 minutes until gently browned and soft.
6. Now prep the remaining parts of the salad before cooking the chicken: first, fill your serving dish with the rocket.
7. Chop the goat's cheese into 1cm-thick rounds and then into half or quarter moons. Sprinkle over the rocket. Add 2 tablespoons of The SP Green Goddess Dressing and gently toss.
8. Next, halve the tomatoes and scatter on top. Add the Quick Pickled Onions to the mix.
9. Now cook the chicken: heat 1 teaspoon of sesame oil in a frying pan over a medium–high heat and, once hot, add the chicken thighs using tongs, leaving any excess marinade in the mixing bowl for now. As you place the thighs in the pan, use the tongs to flatten them into the pan so they caramelise on the outside. Continuously flip the thighs – every 30 seconds or so – to help caramelise the sauce on the outside. After 7 minutes, add the remaining marinade from the mixing bowl and increase

2 tbsp soft dark brown sugar
1 tsp sriracha
1 tsp white miso paste
1 tbsp tamari
½ lime (juice)
2 tsp toasted sesame oil
4 chicken thighs, skinless and boneless (550g)
1 large sweet potato
1 sprig of rosemary
1 tbsp extra virgin olive oil
¼ tsp garlic granules
1 tsp sea salt
2 handfuls of rocket, rinsed and dried
120g goat's cheese
15 cherry tomatoes

READY TO ROCK:

6 tbsp The SP Green Goddess Dressing (see page 118)

4 tbsp Quick Pickled Onions (see page 28)

5–6 tbsp Maple Walnuts (see page 24) or toasted plain walnuts – but you won't quite feel the full magic

the heat to high. Leave the chicken still for a minute or so while the marinade caramelises and becomes thick and sticky, then turn over with tongs a couple of times to make sure the marinade sticks to both sides. Remove from the pan and place on a chopping board to rest for a couple of minutes, then slice and arrange on top of your salad.

10. Dress with 4 tablespoons of The SP Green Goddess Dressing, then finish with the Maple Walnuts or toasted walnuts.

TIP:

For the perfect plant-based GOAT, preheat the oven to 200°C/180°C fan. Cut 4 portobello mushrooms into slices and dress with 2 tsp tamari, 2 tsp maple syrup, 1 tsp balsamic vinegar, 1 tsp olive oil and the leaves of 3 sprigs of thyme. Add a drained and rinsed 400g tin of chickpeas and a pinch of sea salt, then transfer to a roasting tray. Roast for 15 minutes before stirring and returning to the oven for 10 more minutes, until deeply golden. Substitute this for the chicken, and swap out the goat's cheese for a plant-based stracciatella.

Clem's Potato Salad
With The SP Green Goddess Dressing

Serves 2

+ Long-Build

This is a salad I'm very proud to have bear my name. It reminds me of al fresco dining in the sunshine, bringing together some classic Italian flavours with the humble British potato – and a jammy egg for good measure. It's a great example of where letting the dressing do the talking saves you a lot of faff, because you can chuck this delicious, nourishing salad together in the time it takes to cook the potatoes.

1. Preheat the oven to 220°C/200°C fan.
2. Halve or quarter the potatoes and place into a roasting tray in a single layer, with 2 tablespoons of olive oil, a good grind of pepper and a generous pinch of sea salt. Toss to coat the potatoes. Slice the top off the bulb of garlic to reveal the tops of the cloves, and place on a piece of foil. Drizzle with 1 teaspoon of olive oil and a pinch of sea salt, then close the foil loosely around the garlic bulb. Place the garlic package onto the tray with the potatoes, and place in the oven for 25 minutes, shaking the potatoes after 15 minutes to stop them from sticking.
3. Meanwhile, bring a large saucepan of salted water to a boil over a medium–high heat. Add the eggs and cook for 6½ minutes. Place an empty bowl under the tap. Once your eggs have finished cooking, carefully transfer them into the bowl and run the cold water tap for 3–4 minutes until the eggs stop cooking in their residual heat. Alternatively, place them in an ice bath.
4. Use a vegetable peeler to peel strands of courgette into a sieve. Sprinkle with a pinch of sea salt and leave over a bowl to draw out some water.
5. Cover your serving dish with the rocket and basil leaves.
6. Slice the radishes into rounds and place in some ice-cold water to crisp up.
7. Drain the sun-dried tomatoes and spread over the rocket and basil base. Dress with 2 tablespoons of The SP Green Goddess Dressing.
8. Finely chop the mint leaves, then squeeze out any excess liquid from the courgette ribbons. Place both together in a bowl and grate in the lemon zest. Use your hands to mix the mint and zest through the courgettes, then separate the ribbons over the salad base you've started building.
9. Defrost the peas in a bowl of hot or boiling water for a couple of minutes, then drain and set aside.
10. Once the potatoes are cooked, allow them to cool slightly, then open the garlic foil packet and gently squeeze out the roasted cloves into the potato tray. Add the drained peas, along with 5 tablespoons of The SP Green Goddess Dressing, and fold it all together.
11. Using a vegetable peeler to create strands, flake in your Parmesan or vegetarian cheese and fold again. Lay the potato salad onto the dressed base of rocket and tomatoes, and scatter the radishes and pine nuts on top. Peel and halve or slice the eggs and dot over the potatoes.

Ingredients
250g new or baby potatoes
2 tbsp + 1 tsp extra virgin olive oil
1 whole garlic bulb
1 tbsp fine cooking salt
2 eggs
1 courgette
Handful of rocket, rinsed and dried
10–12 basil leaves, plus extra to garnish
Handful of radishes
100g sun-dried tomatoes
10 mint leaves
½ lemon (zest)
100g frozen peas
40g Parmesan or vegetarian hard cheese, plus extra to garnish
80g toasted pine nuts
Sea salt and black pepper

READY TO ROCK:

7 tbsp The SP Green Goddess Dressing (see page 118)

TIP:

If you'd like to add a 'protein premium' here, serve this up as a bed for some roasted cod, or some flaked smoked mackerel.

Green Tahini Dressing

Dresses 4–6 salads

We owe thanks to the queen of tahini, Christina Soteriou, for this recipe. This was the dressing we designed for a menu partnership we ran with her, and it proved so popular we made it a mainstay item. A silky smooth tahini drizzle underpinned by super-fresh East Asian flavours that you'll want to pour on everything – from the tofu knots we share on page 125, to Roasted Aubergine, Spicy Cashew Chickpeas + Kale on page 178. Thank you, Christina, for sharing your unrivalled power over tahini.

25g fresh ginger
65g fresh coriander
120g tahini
1 tbsp white miso paste
1 tsp agave
120ml water
¼ tsp sea salt

1. Peel your ginger using the edge of a teaspoon and finely chop.
2. Chop the thick stems from the ends of the coriander and discard, then add the leaves and the remaining parts of the stems to your blender.
3. Add the remaining ingredients and blitz until completely smooth. Store in an airtight jar or container in the fridge for up to 1 week.

TRY IT WITH:

+ Roasted Salmon with Bean Sprouts + Lime Leaf Shred (see page 158)
+ Curly 'n' Cold Harissa Noodles with Sesame Squash (see page 173)
+ Roasted Aubergine, Spicy Cashew Chickpeas + Kale (see page 178)

Christina Soteriou's Tofu Knot + Toasted Seed Soba Noodle Salad

With Green Tahini Dressing

Serves 2

+ Long-Build
+ Gut Happy

This is a recipe from a woman with HUGE plant energy. Christina Soteriou knows how to make eating vegetables incredibly exciting, and we owe her our thanks for introducing us to the wonder that is the tofu knot. Tofu knots are made from soy milk that's dried, pressed and twisted into shapes that hold onto flavour immensely well. They are so easy to use, and look so impressive atop any dish. Here we have Christina's Salad Project salad, with chilled noodles, heaps of kimchi and crispy, chewy, sticky tofu knots caramelised in a sauce that combines Middle Eastern and East Asian ingredients. It is a recipe that locks in Christina's title as Queen of Plants. You won't find tofu knots in every supermarket, but they're worth seeking out online for a lot of fun.

Ingredients
150g tofu knots
Pinch of fine cooking salt
100g Tenderstem broccoli
160g soba noodles
15g fresh ginger, peeled
1 garlic clove
4 tbsp toasted sesame oil
2 tbsp mirin
2 tbsp tamari
15g white miso paste
2 tsp maple syrup
¼ + ⅛ tsp cumin seeds
¼ + ⅛ tsp coriander seeds
⅛ tsp fennel seeds
¾ tsp sesame seeds
Handful of baby spinach
1 lime (juice)
Generous serving of kimchi
Small handful of fresh coriander leaves

READY TO ROCK:

5–6 tbsp Green Tahini Dressing (see page 124)

3 tbsp Crispy Chilli Oil (see page 131) or toasted cashews

1. Boil the kettle. Place the tofu knots into a heat-proof bowl and pour over the boiling water until fully immersed, with about 5cm of water above the knots. Set aside for a minimum of 30 minutes.
2. Bring a large saucepan of water to a boil with a pinch of cooking salt. Add the broccoli and cook for 3 minutes. Keeping the water in the pan, use tongs to remove the broccoli from the water and transfer into a sieve. Run under cold water for a couple of minutes (or place in a bowl of iced water), then set aside in a bowl to free up the sieve.
3. Next add your soba noodles to the boiling water and cook for 4 minutes, giving them a swirl around the pan to avoid sticking. Strain the noodles in the sieve and run under a constant stream of cold water, using tongs, and (once cooler!) your fingers to wash off the starch and stop the noodles from sticking. Set aside in a bowl.
4. Into a blender, measure the ginger, garlic, 2 tablespoons of sesame oil, mirin, tamari, miso paste and maple syrup, and blitz until smooth and fully combined.
5. In a dry frying pan, toast the cumin seeds, coriander seeds, fennel seeds and sesame seeds over a gentle heat for 3–4 minutes until you start smelling the aromatics being released.
6. Pour three-quarters of the toasted seeds (saving the rest for later) into the mixture in the blender and pulse once or twice to slightly crack the spices into the mixture, without fully blending. Don't wash the frying pan; you'll use it again.
7. Drain the soaked tofu knots in the sieve and squeeze hard to remove any excess water. Heat the remaining 2 tablespoons of sesame oil in the frying pan over a medium–high heat and add the tofu knots. Fry in the oil until crisp and golden on the outside, using tongs to turn them over every few minutes – this should take around 6–7 minutes to colour well. Once

HERBY

golden, reduce the heat a little and add the sauce from the blender. While it bubbles, keep swirling the pan to coat the tofu knots in the sauce as it thickens and caramelises. Keep going until all the sauce is coating the tofu knots and they are sticky and glistening.

8. Start building the salad by dressing the noodles with 3–4 tablespoons of Green Tahini Dressing. Cover the base of your serving bowl or plate with the baby spinach and dress with a squeeze of lime. Pour the noodles on top, either all over, or in one corner of the dish. Next, layer on your broccoli, followed by the kimchi. Use tongs to add the sticky tofu knots and sprinkle with the reserved toasted seeds. Drizzle the whole salad with another 2 tablespoons of Green Tahini Dressing, before topping with Crispy Chilli Oil or toasted cashews and the coriander leaves. Serve with a final squeeze of lime.

TIP:

If you can't find tofu knots, just sub in super-firm tofu, marinate it in the tofu knot sauce for 15 minutes, then fry in toasted sesame oil. Add the remaining marinade to caramelise once the tofu has crisped up.

Crispy Mushroom + Smacked Cucumber Rice Bowl

With Green Tahini Dressing

Serves 2

+ Medium-Build
+ Protein Power

A seriously satisfying rice bowl, loaded up with colours, textures and heaps of umami flavour. Crispy, earthy mushrooms are the perfect partner to our Green Tahini's herby zing, while brown rice provides a spoon-worthy base to its creamy weight. The soft-boiled eggs can easily be skipped to make this a plant-based power bowl.

1. Preheat the oven to 200°C/180°C fan.
2. Weigh the brown rice into a saucepan and measure in the water. Stir through ¼ teaspoon of cooking salt. Bring the water to a boil over a medium-high heat, then place a lid on the pot and reduce the heat to medium. Allow to simmer until the rice is cooked – roughly 25 minutes. (Simply add more water if it dries out and isn't fully cooked.)
3. In a large bowl, combine the maple syrup, 2 tablespoons of the tamari or soy sauce, 1 tablespoon of the sesame oil, the balsamic vinegar and the miso paste. Slice the mushrooms into 1–2cm strips, then coat well with the marinade. Add the rinsed chickpeas and mix again. Set aside.
4. Use a mandolin or knife to finely slice the radishes into rounds. Place into a bowl with 2 tablespoons of the rice vinegar, ¼ teaspoon of cooking salt and ¼ teaspoon of caster sugar. Add enough water to cover, and stir to dissolve the sugar and salt. Set aside to pickle.
5. Place the mushrooms and chickpeas onto a parchment-lined baking sheet and roast for 15 minutes, then stir and return to the oven for 10–15 minutes until deep in colour and crispy round the edges.
6. Remove the end of the cucumber half, then use a rolling pin to smack the cucumber until it splits. Roughly chop the split cucumber pieces into diagonal chunks, scooping up and discarding any loose clumps of seeds. Place into a bowl and sprinkle with a pinch of cooking salt and a pinch of caster sugar. Set aside to expel excess liquid.
7. Empty the cooked rice into a serving dish and fold through the spinach. Drizzle with 2 tablespoons of Green Tahini Dressing.
8. Fill the saucepan with water and bring to a boil with a large pinch of cooking salt. Add your eggs and leave to boil for 6 minutes (runny) or 7 minutes (jammy), then remove and place into a bowl of cold water.
9. Strain off the cucumber liquid and dress the smacked cucumber with 1 teaspoon of the tamari, 1 teaspoon of the rice vinegar, ½ teaspoon of the sesame oil and either the Crispy Chilli Oil or chilli flakes.
10. Onto the rice base, build your avocado, pickled radish, smacked cucumber and roasted mushrooms into their own sections. Dress with 2 tablespoons of Green Tahini Dressing. Peel and halve the boiled eggs, placing on top of the salad. Finish by chopping the roasted peanuts and sprinkling on top with a generous squeeze of lime. Serve with extra dressing if needed.

125g short grain brown rice

500ml water

Fine cooking salt

1 tbsp maple syrup

2 tbsp + 1 tsp tamari (if gluten-free) or light soy sauce

1 tbsp + ½ tsp toasted sesame oil

1 tsp balsamic vinegar

1 tsp white miso paste

200g mushrooms (preferably oyster, shiitake or portobello)

200g (drained weight) jarred or tinned chickpeas (preferably the large Spanish chickpeas from a jar), drained and rinsed

10–15 radishes

2 tbsp + 1 tsp rice wine vinegar

Caster sugar

½ cucumber

Handful of baby spinach

2 eggs

1 ripe avocado, sliced

80g roasted, salted peanuts

½ lime (juice)

READY TO ROCK:

4 tbsp Green Tahini Dressing (see page 124), plus extra if needed

1 tbsp Crispy Chilli Oil (see page 31 or ¼ tsp crushed red chilli flakes

TIP:

Double up your smacked cucumber and keep it in the fridge, dressed. It will get better with time spent in its marinade and can be used in lots of other salads.

HERBY

Caper + Dill Dressing

Dresses 4–6 salads

Both capers and dill can divide opinion, and this recipe is pretty punchy with both. But if you're open to conversion, maybe we can help you with our pitch for capers' awesome versatility ... Chuck them into a panzanella with some of their salty brine, fold them through a creamy potato salad or crisp them up in the oven with some breadcrumbs and sprinkle them on anything – the options are endless.

50g dill

40g capers, drained

1 tsp runny honey

2 tsp Dijon mustard

2 lemons (zest and juice)

50ml apple cider vinegar

100ml extra virgin olive oil

Sea salt, to taste (optional)

1. Chop off the thickest part of the dill stems and discard, then place the remainder of the sprigs into a high-speed blender. Add the remaining ingredients and use the pulse setting to create a chunky dressing.
2. Taste and add salt, if needed. Store in an airtight jar or container in the fridge for up to 1 week.

TRY IT WITH:

+ Crispy Spiced Lamb, Aubergine + Freekeh with Pickled Onions (see page 100)
+ Garlic + Thyme Chicken, Butter Bean + Sun-Dried Tomato (see page 89)

Crispy New Potatoes, Whipped Ricotta + Pickled Radish

With Caper + Dill Dressing

Serves 2

+ Medium-Build

One of the (many) beautiful things about salad is that sometimes you throw something together accidentally that quite literally takes your breath away. This recipe appeared out of nowhere in a moment of mania while writing this book. We thought it was so stunning it deserved a spot in the book (and hopefully on future menus). Chic, colourful, cool, comforting and characterful – everything we can hope for from Salad Project salads. Oh, except customised, which you can add to that list by taking this recipe as your base and chucking in some smoked mackerel, leftover roast chicken or a jar of beans.

1. Preheat the oven to 220°C/200°C fan.
2. Put the potatoes into a roasting tray. If some are much bigger than others, halve them. Otherwise, leave them whole. Add 3 tablespoons of the olive oil, the pepper and 2 generous pinches of sea salt. Use your hands to give the potatoes a good coating. Roast in the oven for 30 minutes.
3. Finely slice the radishes, using a knife or a mandolin. Place in a small bowl or jar with the white wine vinegar, ⅛ teaspoon fine cooking salt and caster sugar. Add water until the radishes are submerged, then give everything a good stir or shake to dissolve the salt and sugar.
4. Next, whip the ricotta. Take a medium mixing bowl and add your ricotta, honey, ¼ teaspoon fine cooking salt, 1 tablespoon of the olive oil and the lemon zest. Use a whisk to whip until relatively smooth – taste, and add a good pinch of sea salt to adjust the flavour. Spread the ricotta across the serving plate, drizzle with 2 tablespoons of the Dill + Caper Dressing and set aside.
5. Meanwhile, take another small roasting tray and add your broccoli, along with 1 teaspoon of the olive oil and a pinch of sea salt. If your pine nuts aren't pre-toasted, whack them into the tray with the broccoli and roast both for 8 minutes.
6. Once your potatoes have been roasting for 30 minutes, remove the tray and use the bottom of a jar to give each potato a good squish until the skin bursts and you have little potato discs. Turn them over, add an extra drizzle of olive oil, then boost the temperature to 250°C/230°C fan and return them to the oven for a final 10 minutes to crisp up in the rising heat.
7. Scatter your potatoes over the whipped ricotta and drizzle a zigzag of honey over them, then layer on your broccoli and pine nuts. Dress with 4 tablespoons of Dill + Caper Dressing and finish by dotting your pink pickled radishes over the top.

Ingredients
600g new or baby potatoes
4 tbsp + 1 tsp extra virgin olive oil, plus extra for drizzling
10 good grinds of pepper
4 radishes
4 tbsp white wine vinegar
⅛ tsp + ¼ tsp fine cooking salt
¼ tsp caster sugar
250g ricotta
1 tsp runny honey
½ lemon (zest)
100g Tenderstem broccoli
80g toasted pine nuts
Sea salt

READY TO ROCK:

6 tbsp Dill + Caper Dressing (see page 130)

TIP:

If you want to add a little extra protein to this dish, I'd highly recommend flaking over some smoked mackerel fillets.

The Spring Fling
With Caper + Dill Dressing

Serves 2

+ Quick-Build
+ Brain + Body Fuel

Capers, dill and smoked salmon really are a holy trinity: something we discovered when three rather strapping Italian brothers dropped a kilo of smoked salmon trimmings at the door of our test kitchen one April. Our hearts (or at least mine) were a-racing, and it's safe to say we were quick to lock in a partnership with their smokehouse for a spring special that epitomises everything that's at its best at this time of year. This is a really satisfying, super-fresh salad that's loaded with the brightest flavours of spring. I just wonder where we got the name from …

1. Preheat the oven to 220°C/200°C fan.
2. Halve or quarter the potatoes, depending on their size and your preference. Place them into a roasting tray big enough to fit them in a single layer and add the olive oil, a couple of pinches of sea salt and a grind of black pepper. Use your hands to coat the potatoes.
3. While waiting for the oven to heat up, use a knife or mandolin to thinly slice the cucumber into 1–2mm slices and place into a jar or airtight container. Add the fine cooking salt, sugar, dill, white wine vinegar and water, and give it a good stir (or shake) until the sugar and salt dissolve.
4. Pop the potatoes into the oven for 15 minutes.
5. Trim the bottom 2.5cm off your asparagus stems and then slice each stem, at an angle, into 3 pieces.
6. After 15 minutes, remove the potatoes from the oven and carefully add the asparagus and capers. Shake and return the tray to the oven for 8 minutes more until the potatoes are crisp and golden.
7. Fill your serving plate with a mix of the baby spinach and cress or rocket. Dress the leaves with 2 tablespoons of Caper + Dill Dressing and toss gently to coat.
8. Remove the smoked salmon from its packet and slice to your preferred size. Grate the zest of the lemon into a small bowl and set aside, then halve the citrus and squeeze one half over the salmon. Grind over some black pepper to finish.
9. Dot the quick pickled cucumbers over the dressed leaves, then add the salmon, folding or rolling each piece instead of just laying it flat.
10. Once the potatoes and asparagus are cooked, add the horseradish sauce and mayonnaise to the tray and use a spoon to coat the mixture well. Finish by folding through the lemon zest. Pile the potatoes onto the salad, drizzle the salad all over with 3–4 tablespoons of Dill + Caper Dressing and finish by sprinkling over the Crispy Onions and some more dill to garnish.

Ingredients
250g new potatoes
1½ tbsp extra virgin olive oil
¼ cucumber
¼ tsp fine cooking salt
½ tsp caster sugar
Small handful of dill, chopped, plus extra to garnish
2 tbsp white wine vinegar
60ml water
6 asparagus stems
1 tbsp capers, drained
Handful of baby spinach
Handful of land cress, watercress or rocket, rinsed and dried
100g smoked salmon
1 lemon (juice of ½ and zest of whole)
1½ tbsp horseradish sauce
1 tsp mayonnaise
Sea salt and black pepper

READY TO ROCK:

5–6 tbsp Caper + Dill Dressing (see page 130)

3 tbsp Crispy Onions (see page 24 for home-made, or shop-bought works fine)

TIP:

This is delicious with roasted salmon fillets, too – particularly the smoked fillets you can find in supermarkets. Roast in the oven for 12 minutes at 200°C/180°C fan.

Salsa Verde

Dresses 4–6 salads

While traditionalists might not call this a 'salad dressing' by definition, we've never been ones to stick to convention at The Salad Project. A secret flavour weapon to have on hand when life's at its busiest, this vibrant green and caper-loaded salsa verde will get you out of many midweek dinner conundrums. Give it a go on our recipes, or just use it to zhuzh up eggs on toast if that's all you have the energy for right now. We've been there. But regardless of your energy levels when you're whipping this up, please stick to some good-quality extra virgin olive oil – you'll reap the antioxidative health (and flavour) benefits three-, four-, eight- or even ten-fold (depending on which you buy).

20g flat leaf parsley
15g basil
2 tbsp capers, drained
2 tsp Dijon mustard
2 tbsp white wine vinegar
120ml extra virgin olive oil
Sea salt and black pepper

1. Place your parsley and basil onto a chopping board. Remove the bottom 1cm from the stems and discard, then roughly chop the rest. Add your capers to the herbs and chop again until the capers are roughly in quarters.
2. Place your herbs and capers into a bowl or a blender. Add the mustard, white wine vinegar, a large pinch of sea salt and a good grind of pepper. Stir with a spoon to combine.
3. Next add the olive oil and either stir well for a chunky sauce, or pulse for 1 second at a time until you reach the desired consistency (I prefer a little texture, so I would avoid blending until completely smooth!). Store in an airtight jar or container in the fridge for up to 1 week. The herbs at the top will fade in colour from oxidation, so give it a good stir before using.

TRY IT WITH:

+ The GOAT (see page 119)
+ Spiced Cauliflower with Smoky Toasted Almonds + Hot Honey Labneh (see page 95)
+ Whole-Spice Lamb Meatballs, Preserved Lemon + Butter Bean Salad (see page 174)

Burrata + Spring
With Salsa Verde

Serves 2

+ Quick-Build

HERBY

This salad delivers what it says on the tin. Our spring favourites – asparagus and pink, cheek-puckering rhubarb – with a creamy crowd-pleaser. If you're not a fan of rhubarb, you can still tuck in to this great combo. Simply ditch the rhubarb, or swap it out for something else like beetroot, artichoke hearts or grilled peach. If you're in the market for a slightly more energy-boosting salad, but like the sound of these flavours, it works great with a base of lemony quinoa.

1. Preheat the oven to 220°C/200°C fan.
2. Trim the bottom 2.5cm off the asparagus and discard. If using thick asparagus, slice down the middle lengthways. If using quite thin asparagus, leave it whole. Place into a parchment-lined roasting tray and drizzle with 1 teaspoon of the olive oil and a pinch of sea salt. Roast in the oven for 8 minutes.
3. Top and tail the radishes and thinly slice them to give you complete circles, either using a knife or a mandolin. Fill a bowl with iced water and place the sliced radishes in here to crisp up.
4. Slice your rhubarb, if using, at an angle into 7cm pieces – you'll use the asparagus tray and parchment paper to roast this once it is free.
5. Meanwhile, pile the mint leaves roughly on top of each other and roll up like a pancake. Thinly slice from one end to the other to give you a fine shred.
6. Slice the chilli into super-fine rings from tip to top, removing the seeds, and set aside.
7. Pile your rocket or lamb's lettuce onto a serving plate and sprinkle on the mint. Add 2 tablespoons of Salsa Verde and toss gently with your hands to coat. Sprinkle over the crisp radish rings and the roasted asparagus.
8. Place the rhubarb into the empty asparagus tray (taking care, as it will still be hot!) and sprinkle with sea salt and 1 teaspoon of the olive oil. Place in the oven for 4 minutes to soften without turning to mush.
9. Once cooked, dot the rhubarb over the salad and then lay your burrata over the top. Gently tear open the burrata to help spread once served, and dress everything with 4 tablespoons of Salsa Verde. Finish with the sliced chilli, Toasted Furikake Seeds and the lemon zest grated all over the salad.

125g asparagus

2 tsp extra virgin olive oil

6 radishes

1 stem of forced rhubarb (optional)

20 mint leaves

1 red chilli

2 handfuls of rocket or lamb's lettuce, rinsed and dried

150g burrata

1 lemon (zest)

Sea salt

READY TO ROCK:

6 tbsp Salsa Verde (see page 136)

8 tbsp Toasted Furikake Seeds (see page 25)

TIP:

Remove the rhubarb and you have a gorgeous mix of veg to fold through some linguine; just be sure to top it with the burrata and dress with lashings of Salsa Verde and extra virgin olive oil.

Steak, Sweet Potato + Rocket Salad
With Salsa Verde

Serves 2

+ Medium-Build

We like to think of ourselves as helping redefine the stereotypes of salad, which often means finding all of the most unanimously popular ingredients (for non-plant-based cooks, in this case!) and chucking them all together. Voilà: delicious, crowd-pleasing salad. This is the result of that philosophy – a recipe that takes a pub dinner (steak and sweet potato fries) and turns it into a really bloody delicious salad that happens to be boosted with antioxidative polyphenols, Vitamin A's precursor, beta-carotene, and lean protein. It's recommended we keep red meat consumption to a weekly or monthly treat, so this is a great recipe for packing in some delicious plants on the side to really make the most of every bite.

1. Preheat the oven 200°C/180°C fan.
2. Remove the steak(s) from any packaging and place onto a plate. Drizzle with 1 tablespoon of the olive oil for each steak, and rub both sides with a generous pinch of sea salt and a hefty grind of pepper. Leave to come to room temperature.
3. Slice the sweet potatoes into 2cm-thick rounds, then cut the rounds into quarters or sixths, depending on the circumference of the vegetable. Place into a large roasting tray, in a single layer, and drizzle with the remaining olive oil. Sprinkle with 1 teaspoon of sea salt, then use your hands to fully coat the sweet potatoes. Roast in the oven for 30 minutes.
4. Cover a serving plate with the rocket and dress with 3 tablespoons of Salsa Verde.
5. Halve the tomatoes and scatter across the rocket.
6. Heat a dry frying pan over a medium–high heat. While the pan is heating, place a cereal bowl upside down on a lipped plate. When the pan is searing hot, use metal tongs to place the steak(s) onto the pan and push the meat the pan to stop it from curling. Leave the steak(s) still for 3 minutes to caramelise before flipping onto the other side for a further 3 minutes. (This will give you a rare steak. Add a couple of minutes to each side if you prefer your steak less rare.) Drape the cooked steak(s) over the upturned bowl to allow the juices to run off. Leave to rest over the bowl for at least 10 minutes.
7. Remove the sweet potatoes from the oven and mix in with the rocket and tomatoes.
8. Slice the steak(s) at an angle across the grain and sprinkle with sea salt. Lay over the salad and dress with 3 tablespoons of Salsa Verde. Use a vegetable peeler to flake the Parmesan over the salad, or use a fine grater for a denser dusting. Top with Crispy Onions.

Ingredients
1–2 rump steak(s) (about 255–500g)
3–4 tbsp extra virgin olive oil
4 small or 2 medium/large sweet potatoes
60g rocket, rinsed and dried
20 plum or cherry tomatoes
50g Parmesan
Sea salt and black pepper

READY TO ROCK:

6 tbsp Salsa Verde (see page 136)

Generous sprinkling of Crispy Onions (see page 28 for home-made, or shop-bought works fine)

TIP:

Build your salad on a big platter – presenting steak this way can mean you actually need less of it than you think, so you can save some to zhuzh up some of the other salads in this book later in the week.

HERBY

Fresh Mint Drizzle

Dresses 4–6 salads

We have a love-hate relationship with mint at The Salad Project. Mint leaves can sometimes be a little intense to chew on whole, and tend to brown easily. So this is our way of incorporating what we love about mint – freshness! – into so many different dishes without the hassle. A crisp, minty fresh drizzle that can be spiced up or spiced down, depending on what you're pairing it with. It's a fridge staple for everything from salads to Sunday roasts …

1. Place all of your ingredients into a blender and blitz until smooth.
2. Taste and dial up the chilli to taste.

Ingredients
30g mint, leaves picked
120g natural yoghurt or plant-based alternative
2 lemons (juice)
2 tsp runny honey or agave
40ml extra virgin olive oil
½ tsp chilli flakes, plus extra to taste (optional)
Grinding of black pepper
1 tsp sea salt

TRY IT WITH:

+ Sumac Salmon with Honey Carrots, Roasted Tenderstem + Lemony Grains (see page 69)
+ Honey Chicken + Jalapeño Quinoa Salad with Toasted Pine Nuts + Tenderstem (see page 148)

Green 'n' Minty Whole Grain Pasta Salad

With Fresh Mint Drizzle

Serves 2

+ Medium-Build
+ Brain + Body Fuel

HERBY

We're big believers in food as fuel, and salad is definitely the rule, not the exception. This is a great recipe to whip up with that in mind, because all too often we starve our bodies of what they need to keep us performing at our best: slow-releasing carbohydrates. We'd be absolutely nowhere without them, so it's only fair we give them centre stage, whether it's for a bit of a midweek meal-prep lunch or a post-workout refuel when you get home. Here's a hearty whole grain pasta salad serving up seven of your weekly plants that'll keep you feeling energised, without the mid-afternoon or post-exercise slump.

1. Preheat the oven to 200°C/180°C fan.
2. Bring the water to a boil in a large saucepan with the cooking salt. While it's heating up, weigh your pasta and, once boiling, add it to the water. Cook according to the packet instructions.
3. While the pasta cooks, halve the cherry tomatoes and lay, cut side up, on a parchment-lined roasting tray in a single layer. Drizzle with 1 tablespoon of the olive oil and the balsamic vinegar, and sprinkle with a generous pinch of salt plus a generous grinding of pepper.
4. Slice the courgette into discs and laying into a second parchment-lined roasting tray in a single layer. Drizzle with 1 tablespoon of the olive oil and sprinkle with salt and pepper. Place both trays into the oven for 20 minutes until nicely coloured and well roasted.
5. Meanwhile, pile the mint leaves roughly on top of each other and roll up like a pancake. Slice thinly from one end to the other to give you a fine shred.
6. Once the pasta is cooked, drain it and run under cold water, using your hands (once it has cooled slightly!) to separate the pieces and stop it from sticking. Pour the drained pasta into a bowl and add a generous pinch of sea salt, along with 2 tablespoons of Toasted Furikake Seeds, 4 tablespoons of Fresh Mint Drizzle and the shredded mint leaves.
7. Cover a serving plate with the rocket, then drizzle with 1 tablespoon of Fresh Mint Drizzle. Next, layer over your pasta and top with the warm roasted vegetables. Finish with 2 more tablespoons of Fresh Mint Drizzle, the remaining 3 tablespoons of Toasted Furikake Seeds, the lemon zest and a drizzle of olive oil.

1.5 litres water

1 tbsp fine cooking salt

200g whole grain fusilli or other whole grain pasta

12–15 cherry tomatoes

2 tbsp extra virgin olive oil, plus extra for drizzling

1 tbsp balsamic vinegar

1 courgette

4 sprigs of mint, leaves picked

30g rocket, rinsed and dried

1 lemon (zest)

Sea salt and black pepper

READY TO ROCK:

5 tbsp Toasted Furikake Seeds (see page 25) or toasted pumpkin seeds

7 tbsp Fresh Mint Drizzle (see page 140)

TIP:

Experiment with your favourite pasta shapes to see which allows the dressing to cling on the best – we'd recommend something with twists, ridges and/or crevices to catch and carry the flavours.

Peaches + Cream

With Fresh Mint Drizzle

Serves 2

+ Quick-Build

This recipe transports us right back to our second summer of service at The Salad Project. Amid the chaos that often came from muddling our way through the early days of building our salad dream, it was a real comfort. Sweet and sour grilled peaches, a gooey burrata you're pretty sure you shouldn't be eating on a salad, and some spirit-lifting fresh mint – the best salve to a hot and hectic day. This salad came to us for a reason and a season, and we're pretty sure it will be with us for a lifetime.

1. Core the peaches, slice into quarters and place into a small mixing bowl. Dress with 1 tablespoon of olive oil, 2 pinches of sea salt and a grind of pepper. Heat a frying or griddle pan over a medium–high heat. Add the peaches in a single layer, placing them flesh side down on one side. Grill for around 4 minutes on the first side until well coloured before flipping onto the other cut side for another 4 minutes. Once the peaches are nicely caramelised, set aside to cool slightly.
2. Drain and rinse the butter beans in a sieve, then place into a mixing bowl and add 2 tablespoons of Fresh Mint Drizzle, 1 teaspoon of olive oil, the lemon zest and your basil and mint leaves. Stir to combine.
3. Lay the rocket over the serving plate and drizzle with 2 tablespoons of Fresh Mint Drizzle. Pile on the dressed butter beans, followed by the grilled peaches.
4. Finely slice the chilli into rings and sprinkle over the peaches. Lay the burrata on top and gently tear open. Top with 2 tablespoons of Fresh Mint Drizzle, then sprinkle with the Maple Walnuts and the mint leaves for garnish. Finish with a little drizzle of olive oil.

---

3 ripe peaches

1 tbsp + 1 tsp extra virgin olive oil, plus extra for drizzling

570g jar or 400g tin of butter beans

1 lemon (zest)

10 basil leaves

15 mint leaves, plus 5 to garnish

60g rocket, rinsed and dried

½ red chilli

150g burrata

Sea salt and black pepper

READY TO ROCK:

6 tbsp Fresh Mint Drizzle (see page 140)

4 tbsp Maple Walnuts (see page 24)

TIP:

Layer burrata curds (stracciatella), butter beans, grilled peaches and a Maple Walnut into a radicchio leaf, drizzle with Fresh Mint Drizzle and garnish with a slice of chilli – a very sexy canapé for your next dinner party.

Real-Deal Green Goddess

Dresses 4–6 salads

HERBY

We dangled the definition of a real-deal Green Goddess dressing on page 118, so it would be rude not to give you a recipe and allow you to make up your own mind which you prefer. In all honesty, it's a completely different vibe of dressing, and there's plenty of room at the top, as they say. This is a silky smooth, super-versatile green drizzle that's essentially a salad in itself. It's built from classic flavours, and you can play with the herb combos however you like, so it'll be a great friend to so many salads.

1. Place the avocado flesh into a blender.
2. Pick the mint leaves from the stems and add to the blender. Chop and discard the bottom 5cm from the basil and coriander stems, and place the rest into the blender.
3. Peel and roughly chop your garlic and add to the blender. Add the remaining ingredients, then blend it all together until silky smooth. Store in an airtight jar or container in the fridge for up to 1 week.

1 ripe avocado

Small handful of mint leaves

Small handful of basil

Small handful of fresh coriander

1 garlic clove

3 limes (juice of 3, zest of 1)

70g natural yoghurt or coconut yoghurt

2 tsp Dijon mustard

60ml extra virgin olive oil

50ml water

½ tsp sea salt

Good grinding of black pepper

TRY IT WITH:

+ A Spoonful of Goodness Salad (see page 108)
+ Green 'n' Minty Whole Grain Pasta Salad (see page 142)
+ The Prawn Star (see page 38)

Honey Chicken + Jalapeño Quinoa Salad with Toasted Pine Nuts + Tenderstem

With Real-Deal Green Goddess

Serves 2
+ Medium-Build
+ Protein Power

This is the salad-ification of the most popular girl at school. Loaded with super green goddess goodness that's tempered with some crowd favourites, from toasted pine nuts to Parmesan, it delivers on both appearance and substance. Give it a go to see just how easy it is to whip up, and how you'll struggle to find meat-eaters who don't want to befriend this green (but not too green) people-pleaser. Why? Because it's wholesome, hearty, fresh and multi-textured.

1. Preheat the oven to 220°C/200°C fan.
2. In a medium-sized bowl, mix the garlic granules with 6 grinds of black pepper and 1 teaspoon of sea salt, along with the olive oil, honey and oregano. Add the chicken thighs and coat completely in the marinade. Set aside at room temperature.
3. Put the quinoa, water and cooking salt into a saucepan and bring to a boil. Once boiling, slightly reduce the heat and allow to cook until the water is absorbed and the quinoa is soft – roughly 15 minutes.
4. Place the Tenderstem broccoli into a roasting tray and drizzle with a little olive oil, then season with sea salt and black pepper. Make space in the middle of the tray and add the marinated chicken thighs, skin side up. Roast in the oven for 8 minutes, then remove the broccoli and set aside. Baste the chicken with any leftover marinade and juices, and roast for a further 10 minutes.
5. Pull the soft lettuce leaves apart, rinse and dry well before spreading over a serving plate and dressing with 3 tablespoons of Real-Deal Green Goddess. Toss with your hands to coat.
6. Once it's cooked, spoon the quinoa over the lettuce leaves, then top with the roasted broccoli and the jalapeños, reserving a couple for garnish. Scatter over half of the fresh herbs.
7. When the chicken is cooked through and nicely golden on top, let it sit for a few minutes before slicing and scattering over the salad. Grate the Parmesan all over the salad, then sprinkle over the toasted pine nuts. Dress with 3 more tablespoons of Real-Deal Green Goddess, and finish with the remaining fresh herbs and a couple more jalapeño slices.

---

1 tsp garlic granules

1 tbsp extra virgin olive oil, plus extra for drizzling

1 tsp runny honey

½ tsp dried oregano

3–4 boneless chicken thighs, skin on

100g mixed-colour quinoa

350ml water

¼ tsp fine cooking salt

100g Tenderstem broccoli

½ oak leaf or butterhead lettuce

3 tbsp jalapeños in brine, drained

Small handful of fresh oregano

Large handful of basil

60g Parmesan

60g toasted pine nuts

Sea salt and black pepper

READY TO ROCK:

6 tbsp Real-Deal Green Goddess (see page 146)

TIP:

Veggies: swap out the chicken for some sliced mushrooms, tossed in the same marinade with an extra tablespoon of olive oil and 1 teaspoon balsamic vinegar, then roasted at 220°C/200°C fan for 20–30 minutes until deeply coloured. Sub the Parmesan for a vegetarian hard cheese, or skip it all together. Pescatarians: swap in some salmon and this combination still slaps.

Green Godd-Eggs-On-Toast
With Real-Deal Green Goddess

Serves 2

+ Quick-Build
+ Protein Power

America is the source of many a great salad, including those so-called salads that take any protein or vegetable and fold it through mayonnaise. Here, we've taken the Real-Deal Green Goddess dressing and subbed it in for mayonnaise, to give you a green twist on an American 'egg salad'. This should leave you feeling like a goddess (or god), because it delivers all the good stuff, from skin-loving avocado and seeds to gut-loving Quick Pickled Onions, brain-fuelling carbs and protein-filled eggs.

1. Fill a medium saucepan with enough water to cover the eggs and add the fine cooking salt. Bring to a boil, then carefully add the eggs and reduce temperature slightly to avoid overflowing. Cook for 7½ minutes.
2. Meanwhile, separate the baby gem leaves and lay them, whole, over your serving dish. Drizzle with 3 tablespoons of Real-Deal Green Goddess.
3. Slice your cornichons into little rounds.
4. Place an empty bowl under the tap. Once your eggs are cooked, carefully place into the bowl and run the cold water tap so the eggs stop cooking in their residual heat. Alternatively, place them in an ice bath. After a few minutes, peel the eggs and roughly chop them into 1–2cm pieces. Place them into a bowl and then transfer to the fridge for 10 minutes to chill. Note: if you're prepping in advance, you can just chill the boiled eggs in their shells and peel and chop them once fully cool later.
5. Once cool, add 3 tablespoons of Real-Deal Green Goddess to your chopped eggs and mix into a sort of green egg mayonnaise. Add a few good grinds of pepper and a pinch of sea salt. Fold through the chopped cornichons, then spoon the mixture onto your dressed baby gem cups. Top each leaf (or the whole plate if you're not working leaf by leaf) with the Quick Pickled Onions, Toasted Furikake Seeds or toasted pumpkin seeds and chilli flakes.
6. Toast your sourdough bread and butter generously, or drizzle with olive oil. Use your hands to whack a leaf filled with the green goddess egg mayo onto your toast for a nice crunch.

4 eggs

1 tsp fine cooking salt

1 baby gem lettuce, rinsed and dried

10 cornichons

Sprinkle of chilli flakes

3–4 slices of sourdough bread

Salted butter or extra virgin olive oil

Sea salt and black pepper

READY TO ROCK:

6 tbsp Real-Deal Green Goddess (see page 146)

2 tbsp Quick Pickled Onions (see page 28)

3 tbsp Toasted Furikake Seeds (see page 25) or toasted pumpkin seeds

TIP:

This makes for a great sandwich filling. Mix the Green Goddess with the boiled eggs and chuck in any of the other salad ingredients that you fancy. Give it a good mix and pile in between two pieces of wholemeal bread, or inside a baked sweet potato.

Spicy
152-194

Lots of our customers love adding some heat to their salads – from pickled chillies to a sprinkle of Tajín – so over time we've built up a strong repertoire of dressings that distribute a fresh kick throughout our bowls. But don't be put off – these dressings all work without the heat, so you can make them to your liking.

From smoky to sweet spices, there are so many options for introducing a little heat to dressing recipes, many of which capture the flavour of popular cuisines. Here we have a collection of some Salad Project classics – including our Thai Peanut Dressing (see page 180) and our house Hot Sauce (see page 194) – that can spice up any salad.

None of them will blow your head off with heat. Instead, we've used the category 'spicy' to bring together the recipes that incorporate warmth from chilli, mustard or gochujang.

Tone up or tone down the spice levels of these recipes to suit you.

KEY CHARACTERISTIC:

Spicing up salads, subtly or seriously

BEST WHEN:

Dressing up something crisp and cool

BUILD YOUR OWN

Curate your own spicy combinations with this simple formula:

SALT · ACID · FAT · SWEET

Most of our spicy dressings are creamy in texture to soften the intensity of any chillies, so the choice of fat base is important.

Spice does best with a hint of sweetness, so don't forget to add a touch when you are getting creative.

FATS:

+ Full-fat mayonnaise
+ Natural yoghurt
+ Crème fraîche or sour cream
+ Full-fat coconut milk
+ Tahini
+ Peanut butter
+ Cashew butter
+ Toasted sesame oil

SWEETS:

+ Caster sugar
+ Soft light brown sugar
+ Honey or agave
+ Maple syrup
+ Pomegranate molasses
+ Date molasses
+ Mirin

HEAT:

+ Chipotle chilli flakes
+ Chilli flakes
+ Ancho chilli flakes
+ Fresh red and green chillies
+ Gochujang
+ Cayenne pepper
+ Mustard

DOS AND DON'TS FOR SPICY DRESSINGS:

+ Add your spice bit by bit if you don't like too much heat – you can always dial it up, but pulling it back is tricky.
+ Pair spicy dressings with sweet touches in a salad for the perfect balance.
+ Sub in different chillies to add new complex flavours – like using smoky chipotle chilli flakes instead of regular crushed chillies.
+ Don't overdress your salad, as a touch too much heat can overpower the delicate flavours of fresh vegetables.
+ Do pair creamy, spicy dressings with cool, crisp lettuces – or even whack some ice into your dressings to add some instant refreshment.
+ Use your spicy dressings as dips for crudités or crisps – just stir through some mayonnaise or natural yoghurt to thicken if needed.

SPICY

Gochujang, Coconut + Ginger Dressing

Dresses 4–6 salads

This dressing has been a lifeline in busy weeks at The Salad Project. Even if you don't have it to hand, you can make it in the time it takes for some noodles to cook. I use it hot or cold as a dressing for ramen noodles or butter beans – wilt through some spinach or steam some broccoli, and you have a bowl of something nourishing and comforting at the end of a long day.

1. Place your coriander leaves into a blender.
2. Peel the ginger using the edge of a teaspoon and grate into the blender using a microplane or a fine grater.
3. Add the coconut milk or yoghurt. If using coconut milk, give the tin a good shake/stir before using, as you want a thick, white consistency, as opposed to just the water. Add your remaining ingredients and blend until smooth.
4. If you want to dial up the spice, add more gochujang, or chuck in some chilli flakes for a bit of fun. Store in an airtight jar or container in the fridge for up to 1 week.

5g fresh coriander leaves
15g fresh ginger
120ml full-fat coconut milk or coconut yoghurt
40g gochujang paste, plus extra to taste (optional)
1 lime (juice)
1 tbsp tamari
1 tsp white miso paste
2 tsp peanut butter
Chilli flakes (optional)

TRY IT WITH:

+ Chilled Sesame Noodles with Balsamic Mushrooms, Lime Slaw + Toasted Furikake Seeds (see page 57)
+ Thai Me Up (see page 184)

Cold Soba Noodles with Kimchi, Pickled Cucumbers + Sesame Tenderstem

With Gochujang, Coconut + Ginger Dressing

Serves 2

+ Quick-Build
+ Gut Happy

VG SPICY

A seriously good, gut-loving noodle bowl, this is a recipe you can serve hot or cold – either way, we're still claiming it's a salad. These speedy, spiced and silky soba noodles are real comfort meal, and for a while we weren't sure why. Then we learned just how much of the body's serotonin originates in the gut. So, feeding our tums with the very best, from the fermented soybeans in gochujang to the probiotics abundant in kimchi, is at least one great way to help boost your mind and mood. This is self-love in a soba salad, ready in ten minutes.

1. Preheat the oven to 200°C/180°C fan.
2. Take a jar or small airtight container and add the salt, sugar, chopped dill, white wine vinegar and 120ml of the water. Stir to dissolve the salt and sugar. Slice the cucumber as thinly as you can and add to the liquid. Ensure all the cucumber is covered by the pickling liquid, then pop in the fridge for later.
3. Place the Tenderstem broccoli into a roasting tray and drizzle with the sesame oil, then sprinkle with 1 tablespoon of the sesame seeds. Shake to coat evenly, then roast in the oven for 8 minutes.
4. While the broccoli is roasting, bring 1.5 litres of water to a boil in a large saucepan. Once boiling, add the noodles and boil for 4 minutes, swirling them to stop them from sticking.
5. Meanwhile, finely slice the spring onion, at an angle, from root to tip.
6. Drain the noodles in a sieve over the sink and rinse continuously with cold water for 2–3 minutes to remove the starch that will make them sticky, then allow them to cool. Once cool, place in a mixing bowl and add 5 tablespoons of the Gochujang, Coconut + Ginger Dressing, along with the ice cube. Use tongs to coat the noodles well, using the ice cube to add a little water and chill the noodles. Once the noodles are coated, remove the ice cube, then add the remaining tablespoon of sesame seeds and the sliced spring onion. Fold through the noodles.
7. Pour the noodles onto a serving plate and dot over the roasted broccoli and any sesame seeds from the tray, followed by the pickled cucumber and kimchi. Finish with a final tablespoon of Gochujang, Coconut + Ginger Dressing and the coriander leaves.

---

1 tsp fine cooking salt

1 tsp caster sugar

Small handful of dill, chopped

4 tbsp white wine vinegar

120ml + 1.5 litres water

½ cucumber

100g Tenderstem broccoli

1 tsp toasted sesame oil

2 tbsp sesame seeds

160g soba noodles (2 portions)

1 spring onion

1 ice cube

150g kimchi

Small handful of fresh coriander leaves

READY TO ROCK:

6 tbsp Gochujang, Coconut + Ginger Dressing (see page 156)

TIP:

If you aren't vegan, top this with some soft-to-jammy boiled eggs for a protein boost. Boil some salted water in a deep saucepan and add your eggs. Boil for 6½ minutes, then remove from the heat and run under cold water, or place in an ice bath. Peel and slice in half to serve.

SPICY

Roasted Salmon with Bean Sprouts + Lime Leaf Shred

With Gochujang, Coconut + Ginger Dressing

Serves 2

+ Medium-Build
+ Brain + Body Fuel

Gochujang is a great good-mood food thanks to the benefits it offers our guts. For this recipe, we take gut-loving gochujang and add to it the incomparably aromatic magic of lime leaves, a plant used in aromatherapy thanks to the stress-busting citrus aroma of its essential oils. In fact, makrut lime leaves possess so many powers they're worth stocking up on if you're out shopping for this recipe – from anti-ageing properties to insect repellent, this is plant power at its best ... Lest we forget its epic flavour, which works so beautifully in contrast to our punchy gochujang drizzle.

1. Preheat the oven to 220°C/200°C fan. Bring a saucepan of water to a boil.
2. While waiting for the water to boil, line a roasting tray with parchment paper and place your salmon fillets into it. Drizzle 1 tablespoon of Gochujang, Coconut + Ginger Dressing over each salmon fillet and sprinkle generously with sesame seeds. Roast in the oven for 12 minutes.
3. Once the water is boiling, add the bean sprouts and cook for 2 minutes, then drain into a sieve and run under cold water to cool.
4. Shred the red cabbage, either by using a knife and slicing finely, or using a mandolin, and tip into a large mixing bowl.
5. If your edamame beans are frozen, bring a saucepan of water to a boil and add the beans. Cook for 3 minutes before draining and running under cold water for 60 seconds to keep their colour (you can also put the drained beans into a bowl of iced water, if easier). Add to the red cabbage, along with the sugar snaps and bean sprouts.
6. Lay the lime leaves on top of one another, then roll up and finely slice into shreds. Add to the cabbage mix, reserving a few for garnish. Squeeze over the lime juice and add a sprinkle of sea salt. Use your hands to mix well and massage.
7. Cover a serving plate with pea shoots or salad leaves. Pour the cabbage and bean sprout mix over the top and drizzle with 2 tablespoons of Gochujang, Coconut + Ginger dressing.
8. If not using, carefully remove the skin from the salmon fillets, then lay the fillets over the top of the salad. If using the skin, fry the cooked salmon, skin side down, in some sesame oil for a couple of minutes on a high heat to crisp up before laying them over the salad.
9. Dot the sushi ginger over the salad and dress with 1–2 tablespoons of Gochujang, Coconut + Ginger Dressing. Pile on the Crispy Onions and finish with some lime leaf strips.

2 salmon fillets
Pinch of sesame seeds (black ones add great colour here)
100g bean sprouts
⅓ red cabbage
100g edamame beans (fresh or frozen)
100g sugar snap peas
4 makrut lime leaves
1 lime (juice)
Handful of pea shoots or mixed leaves, rinsed and dried
Sesame oil (optional)
15 pieces of pickled sushi ginger
Sea salt

READY TO ROCK:

5–6 tbsp Gochujang, Coconut + Ginger Dressing (see page 156)

2 handfuls of Crispy Onions (see page 24 for home-made, or shop-bought works fine)

TIP:

Swap out the salmon for some aubergine batons. Preheat the oven to 220°C/200°C fan. Brush the aubergine with oil and sprinkle with salt, then cook for 8–10 minutes in a griddle or frying pan. Brush with Gochujang, Coconut + Ginger Dressing and move to a foil-lined roasting tray to roast for 20 minutes, turning halfway through.

SPICY

Thai Vinaigrette

Dresses 4–6 salads

Here's a recipe to reignite your passion for vinaigrettes. That may sound a little strong, but give this one a go. It shakes together some of the punchiest flavours of Thai cooking into one unassuming but taste bud-altering liquid of pure gold – and we think you'll probably agree. Like a Thai dipping sauce, but stretched with a touch of sesame oil, we've used this on pork and prawns here, but it's enough just poured over some cold noodles or rice, or served over steamed greens or some silken tofu.

1. Finely slice or chop your chillies, including the seeds, and place into a jam jar.
2. Peel and crush your garlic using the side of a knife or garlic crusher and add a little sea salt to help turn it into a smooth paste. Add to the jam jar.
3. Add all the remaining ingredients to the jar and seal the lid tightly. Shake well to emulsify. It's best to let the flavours mingle for a few hours before using, if you don't need to use it right away. It'll still have great flavour if you don't have time to wait, though! Keep the jar in the fridge for up to 1 week, shaking vigorously before each use.

2 Thai chillies
1 garlic clove
45g caster sugar
70ml fish sauce
2 limes (juice)
60ml rice wine vinegar
3 tbsp toasted sesame oil

TRY IT WITH:

+ A Spoonful of Goodness Salad (see page 108)
+ Tamari Tofu with Vermicelli Noodles, Cabbage Slaw + Crispy Onions (see page 102)

Aromatic Pork Larb + Noodle Salad with Toasted Peanuts

With Thai Vinaigrette

Serves 2

+ **Medium-Build**
+ **Protein Power**

SPICY

There are moments for thick, glossy dressings, and there are moments for thin vinaigrettes that stop you in your tracks with their aromatic intensity. This is a moment for the latter. Our Thai Vinaigrette turns pork mince into an incomparably refreshing headliner for a flavourful bowl that you'll want to eat with a spoon. In fact, the pork is so tasty, we'd recommend doubling up that part of the recipe and keeping it in an airtight container in the fridge so you can sprinkle it on any leftovers – or even just into a lettuce cup as a quick pick-me-up. Like the vinaigrette, the aromatic pork mince also gets better with time in the fridge to let the flavours mingle.

1. Heat the olive oil in a large frying pan or wok over a medium–high heat and add the pork mince, cooking salt and pepper. Use a wooden spatula to break up the meat so you can get it moving round the pan. Cook for 15 minutes until well coloured and caramelised.
2. Meanwhile, in a small saucepan, combine your sesame oil, lemon grass, chilli, ginger, tamari or soy sauce and fish sauce, and heat through over a medium heat for 5 minutes.
3. Once the pork is well cooked, add this aromatic mixture to the meat, along with the juice of half the lime, and stir to combine. Pour into a bowl, and keep the pan aside for later.
4. Boil the kettle and place the noodles in a heat-proof bowl. Pour the boiling water over the noodles to cover for 2 minutes, then drain and rinse briefly with cold water.
5. Using the pork pan, toast your peanuts over a medium heat, scraping up any juices from the pork into the peanuts. Once lightly toasted, roughly chop the nuts, then mix with a pinch of sea salt.
6. Gently bash the cucumber with the bottom of a jar and scrape out any loose seeds (you don't need to remove all of them), then roughly chop into bite-sized pieces. Tip into a bowl with 2 tablespoons of Thai Vinaigrette. Leave to sit for a couple of minutes.
7. Pull apart the baby gem leaf by leaf and add to a large mixing bowl. Add 2 tablespoons of Thai Vinaigrette and toss gently. Lay onto a serving plate. Pour your noodles over the leaves, either placing some on each leaf if you want separate cups, or just piling them on top for a sharing salad. Top with the pork, followed by the smacked cucumber and Pickled Chillies.
8. Roughly chop the coriander, including the stems.
9. Dress the salad with 2 tablespoons of Thai Vinaigrette and top with the chopped peanuts and coriander. Finish with a squeeze of lime.

Ingredients
1 tbsp extra virgin olive oil
250g pork mince (10% fat)
¼ tsp fine cooking salt
4 grinds of black pepper
1 tbsp toasted sesame oil
1 lemon grass stalk, crushed
1 red chilli, finely chopped
25g fresh ginger, peeled and chopped into matchsticks
2 tbsp tamari or light soy sauce
4 tbsp fish sauce
1 lime (juice)
2 x 150g packs of quick-cook medium wheat noodles
80g unsalted peanuts
½ cucumber
1 baby gem lettuce, rinsed and dried
Large handful of fresh coriander
Sea salt

READY TO ROCK:

6 tbsp Thai Vinaigrette (see page 160)

1 tbsp Pickled Chillies (see page 28) or freshly sliced chillies

TIP:

Make some mini pork larb lettuce cups and lay them on a platter for canapés or picnic snacks.

SPICY

Prawn + Mango Salad with Roasted Sweet Potatoes

With Thai Vinaigrette

Serves 2

+ Medium-Build

A super sunny salad of pinks, oranges and yellows, bursting with aromatic flavours, and over 70 per cent of your daily vitamin C. Boost this bowl with some spinach, and the bountiful vitamin C will help your body make the absolute most of the iron bump that comes with these leafy greens.

1. Preheat the oven to 220°C/200°C fan.
2. Cut the sweet potato into 5–7cm chunks and place onto a roasting tray in a single layer. Drizzle with 1 tablespoon of sesame oil and sprinkle with a generous pinch of sea salt. Roast in the oven for 15–18 minutes until soft.
3. Meanwhile, heat 1 teaspoon of sesame oil in a small frying pan over a medium heat. Add your frozen prawns, plus a pinch of cooking salt, and cook for 5–8 minutes until pink.
4. While the prawns are cooking, you can start preparing the serving plate by covering it with the chopped mango. Squeeze the lime juice over the mango and finish with a pinch of sea salt.
5. When the prawns are done, drain off the cooking liquid and place the prawns in a bowl with 3 tablespoons of Thai Vinaigrette and the leaves from 2 of your mint sprigs, roughly torn.
6. Remove the sweet potatoes from the oven and dot among the mango. Spoon the prawns over the top, then finish with Quick Pickled Onions, another 2–3 tablespoons of Thai Vinaigrette and a few whole leaves from the remaining mint sprig.

1 large sweet potato

1 tbsp + 1 tsp toasted sesame oil

225g frozen raw peeled jumbo king prawns

Pinch of fine cooking salt

450g pre-chopped really ripe mango or 1 really ripe mango, peeled and chopped

½ lime (juice)

3 sprigs of mint, leaves picked

Sea salt

READY TO ROCK:

5–6 tbsp Thai Vinaigrette (see page 160)

2 tbsp Quick Pickled Onions (see page 28)

TIP:

For a heavier meal, load up with some red rice or quinoa tossed in some toasted sesame oil and the juice of half a lime.

SPICY

Miso-Mustard Dressing

Dresses 4–6 salads

If you were to ask me to name the worst dressing we have had on our menu over The Salad Project's history, I would have to say the Honey Mustard. I personally don't think this dressing hits any of the criteria for a good dressing: its honey-sweetness overshadows any kick I'm craving from the mustard and mutes the acidity that all good dressings need to lift a salad to new heights. Here's our rebrand of honey-mustard dressing that pulls together mustard and maple under one roof with our favourite East Asian-inspired flavour bombs: miso, fresh ginger, rice vinegar and tamari. The result? A gorgeously salty-sweet glossy glaze for salads with a sturdier base and a pick-me-up for proteins like roast chicken, turkey, salmon and quinoa.

1 garlic clove
12g fresh ginger
50g white miso paste
25g English mustard
35g wholegrain mustard
45ml maple syrup
25ml rice wine vinegar
3 tbsp tamari or light soy sauce

1. Peel and crush your garlic using the side of a knife or a garlic crusher and a little sea salt to help turn it into a smooth paste.
2. Peel your ginger using the edge of a teaspoon and chop finely.
3. Place the garlic, ginger and all the remaining ingredients into a blender and blitz until smooth.
4. Taste and adjust the thickness by adding a little water, if necessary. Store in an airtight jar or container in the fridge for up to 1 week.

TRY IT WITH:

+ The Market Bowl (see page 84)
+ Roasted Courgette + Burrata Salad with Chickpeas + Garlicky Seeds (see page 90)

Shredded Cabbage with Garlic-Thyme Chicken Thighs + Pomegranate Seeds

With Miso-Mustard Dressing

Serves 2

+ Medium-Build

All too often, we jump to leafy bases for salads when really a sturdier shredded base is a better vehicle for slightly thicker, glossy dressings. The smoky bacon in this salad delivers little flavour bombs when folded through a miso-y cabbage slaw, and the pomegranate seeds add a necessary zing to keep things fresh. If you're so inclined, feel free to cut the cabbage with some other brassicas – like Brussels sprouts. You could even swap out the chicken for some leftover turkey and the pomegranates for zippy cranberries. And just like that, we made Christmas salad ... something we vowed never to do. Oops.

1. Preheat the oven to 220°C/200°C fan.
2. Mix the garlic granules, thyme, sugar, a good grind of pepper and a hefty pinch of sea salt in a medium–large bowl with the olive oil. Add the chicken thighs and use tongs or your hands to ensure the marinade reaches every crevice of the chicken. Set aside for at least 10 minutes.
3. Quarter the cabbage, then use a knife, mandolin or vegetable peeler to slice into thin strands and place onto a serving plate or bowl. Add the lemon juice and 2 pinches of sea salt. Use your fingers to massage the dressed cabbage, then let it sit and soak up the marinade.
4. Place the chicken thighs and all their excess marinade into a roasting tray in a single layer and roast in the oven for 15 minutes.
5. Place the bacon rashers in a single layer in a frying pan over a medium–high heat and cook until crispy, flipping with tongs every few minutes.
6. While the bacon is cooking, use a vegetable peeler to first peel the outer skin off the carrot and discard, and then create nice ribbons to add to the cabbage. Note: If you lay the carrot flat on a board and peel while holding it still, you'll get nice wide ribbons. Once you hit the 'core', just flip onto the other side.
7. Once the chicken has been cooking for 15 minutes, turn each thigh using metal tongs and return to the oven for a further 10 minutes until nicely coloured and cooked through.
8. Once the bacon is crispy, roughly chop it and add to the cabbage and carrot mix. Add 2 tablespoons of Miso-Mustard Dressing and a few grinds of pepper, and mix well.
9. When the chicken is fully cooked, remove it from the tray and let it rest for a couple of minutes on a chopping board.
10. Meanwhile, pour your dressed cabbage and bacon mix onto the serving plate.
11. Slice the chicken and place on top of the cabbage. Top the salad with another 3–4 tablespoons of Miso-Mustard Dressing and scatter over the Maple Walnuts and pomegranate seeds.

Ingredients
1 tsp garlic granules
1 tsp dried thyme
½ tsp soft dark brown sugar
1 tsp extra virgin olive oil
3–4 chicken thighs, skinless and boneless
¼ white cabbage
½ lemon (juice)
4 rashers of smoked, streaky bacon
1 carrot
2 tbsp pomegranate seeds
Sea salt and black pepper

READY TO ROCK:

5–6 tbsp Miso-Mustard Dressing (see page 166 – use tamari if gluten-free)

4 tbsp Maple Walnuts (see page 24)

TIP:

If you want to keep things more savoury, swap the Maple Walnuts out for toasted hazelnuts.

Salty-and-Sweet Cavolo Nero, Quinoa + Black Cherry Salad with Blue Cheese + Maple Walnuts

With Miso-Mustard Dressing

Serves 2

+ Medium-Build

SPICY

Our co-founder, Florian, asks for blue cheese to come back onto the menu every time we run a development cycle, so this one's an homage to him. A super-glossy, late summer salad that's sweet and salty. This is a real joy to throw together – unless you don't like getting your hands dirty, in which case, get someone to stone the cherries for you. There's a lot going on here as it is, but feel free to layer in some personal touches if you want to add a little extra protein. Honey-mustard chicken or some crispy chickpeas would work too.

1. Strip the cavolo nero leaves from the stems and slice into 5–7cm pieces. Place into a bowl and add the sesame oil, massaging the cavolo nero with your hands to slightly soften it.
2. Put the quinoa, water and cooking salt into a saucepan and bring to a boil. Once boiling, slightly reduce the heat and allow to cook until the water is absorbed and the quinoa is soft – roughly 15 minutes.
3. Carefully stone the cherries by using a paring knife to halve them, then pushing out the stone with your fingers. Place them in a bowl and set aside.
4. Next, use a vegetable peeler to peel and discard the outer skin of the carrot and parsnip. Then hold each vegetable flat on a chopping board to peel nice wide ribbons from one side, before flipping the vegetable and repeating on the other side. Add the ribbons to a bowl, toss together with a pinch of sea salt and set aside.
5. Once the quinoa is fully cooked, grate in the lemon zest, and then squeeze in the juice. Add the olive oil and mix to combine. Add the cavolo nero, carrots and parsnips to the quinoa, along with 3 tablespoons of Miso-Mustard Dressing and a pinch of sea salt. Stir to distribute evenly, then pour out onto a serving plate. Sprinkle over the cherries, then use your fingers to crumble the blue cheese evenly over the salad, if using. Finish with an extra tablespoon of Miso-Mustard Dressing and a scattering of Maple Walnuts.

6 cavolo nero leaves, rinsed and dried
1 tbsp toasted sesame oil
100g mixed-colour quinoa
350ml water
¼ tsp fine cooking salt
10 cherries
1 carrot
1 parsnip
½ lemon (zest and juice)
1 tbsp extra virgin olive oil
100g blue cheese (optional)
Sea salt

READY TO ROCK:

4 tbsp Miso-Mustard Dressing (see page 166 – use tamari if gluten-free)

4–5 tbsp Maple Walnuts (see page 24)

TIP:

Swap out the cherries for grilled plums or apple, or just leave them out entirely if you aren't a fan of fruit in salads.

Harissa-Tahini Dressing

SPICY

Dresses 4–6 salads

We've explored using harissa in just about every way we can at The Salad Project – on roasted cauliflower, on chicken, in a labneh ... But whichever way we've played with it, we've always ended up whisking it into some kind of sauce – so here's a harissa dressing that you can keep in your fridge, ready to use as soon as your midweek salad calls for a buzzword to boost its sex appeal.

1. Peel the ginger using the edge of a teaspoon and chop finely or grate.
2. Add the ginger and all remaining ingredients to your blender. Blend until smooth. If the consistency is too thick, add a little more water and blitz again.
3. Taste and adjust salt to your preference. Store in an airtight jar or container in the fridge for up to 1 week.

10g fresh ginger

50g tahini

35g rose harissa

2 tsp chilli flakes (we recommend Aleppo for their milder flavour)

2 tsp runny honey

2 tbsp toasted sesame oil

1 lime (juice)

100ml water, plus extra if needed

1 tsp sea salt, plus extra to taste (optional)

TRY IT WITH:

+ Crispy Spiced Lamb, Aubergine + Freekeh with Pickled Onions (see page 100)
+ Miso Chicken with Crispy Spiced Chickpeas + Pickled Cucumbers (see page 48)

Curly 'n' Cold Harissa Noodles with Sesame Squash

With Harissa-Tahini Dressing

Serves 2

+ Medium-Build

SPICY

'Noodles need not apply' could not be further from our attitude when it comes to choosing carbs to pair with Middle Eastern flavours. In fact, we tend to encourage their presence in so many home-made salads because they're at their absolute best when cooked in small batches, fresh from the hob as a partner to all cuisines. Explore using different types of noodles as the base for your salads – the texture of these curly egg noodles is so satisfying, largely because it stirs memories of Super Noodles whipped up in a cereal bowl with some boiling water. Fast forward a few (...) years and how we fuel ourselves might have changed, but that doesn't mean you can't have a little fun. Food is, after all, best when consumed with a side of nostalgia – and salads don't need to be an exception.

1.5 litres water
1 tsp fine cooking salt
½ butternut squash
1 tbsp toasted sesame oil
3 tbsp sesame seeds
3 nests of fine egg noodles
Small handful of mint
Small handful of fresh coriander
1 spring onion
1 ice cube
Sea salt

READY TO ROCK:

7 tbsp Harissa-Tahini Dressing (see page 72)

1. Preheat the oven to 220°C/200°C fan.
2. Add the water to a saucepan with the fine cooking salt and bring to a boil.
3. Slice your squash into half moons, removing the seeds, but leaving the skin on. Place onto a roasting tray in a single layer and drizzle with the sesame oil, then sprinkle with 1 tablespoon of the sesame seeds and some sea salt. Roughly mix with your hands to coat the squash, then roast for 25 minutes until soft and golden.
4. Once the water is boiling, add your noodle nests and use tongs to separate the strands. Boil for 4 minutes, then drain in a sieve over the sink. Rinse with cold water, using tongs to separate the noodles, and allow them to cool.
5. Use kitchen paper to dry out the saucepan, then add your remaining sesame seeds and toast over a gentle heat until turning golden brown. Pour into a small bowl to stop them burning and allow to cool.
6. While the noodles are cooling, roughly chop the mint and coriander, and slice the spring onion into thin rounds.
7. Place your noodles back into the empty saucepan or tip into a clean mixing bowl, and add 6 tablespoons of Harissa-Tahini Dressing, plus an ice cube. Use the tongs to mix the dressing in. The ice cube will help chill the noodles and add a little water to loosen the mix. Remove the ice cube when the noodles are fully dressed and glossy. Add most of your herbs and spring onion, saving some to sprinkle on top for garnish.
8. Lay the noodles onto a serving dish, then top with the sesame squash, an extra tablespoon of Harissa-Tahini Dressing, the reserved herbs and spring onion, and, finally, your toasted sesame seeds.

TIP:

Depending on your diet, there are lots of noodles to play with. Wholewheat noodles or soba noodles (which are made from buckwheat and are gluten-free) are great options if you're looking for complex carbohydrates that keep your energy levels nice and steady. But white noodles, like udon, don't need to be off-limits, particularly if you're balancing them with some good vegetables and proteins.

Whole-Spice Lamb Meatballs, Preserved Lemon + Butter Bean Salad

With Harissa-Tahini Dressing

Serves 2

+ Medium-Build
+ Protein Power

We never really talk about salads as 'deconstructed', because we always think of building them from the base up. But the best way to describe this salad is to say it's like a pitta that's been torn open with its insides left to fend for themselves. And my god they do, with main-character energy being thrown at you from all sides – from dribble-inducing preserved lemon slices and caramelised lamb meatballs brimming with toasted whole spices to butter beans and the freshest of herbs by the bucketload. Yet, despite this cacophony of epic flavour, this salad delivers perfect harmony – in under 25 minutes.

1. Measure the whole-seed spices and sesame seeds into a dry frying pan and toast over a gentle heat for 2–3 minutes, until fragrant.
2. Place the lamb into a large mixing bowl and add the fine cooking salt, ½ teaspoon of sea salt and the ground spices. Mix well to combine and evenly distribute the spices. Once slightly cooled, add the toasted whole-seed spices and mix again until evenly distributed through the lamb. Roll the mixture into small 2.5cm meatballs.
3. In the frying pan used for toasting the spices, heat 2 tablespoons of olive oil over a medium heat and then, using tongs, start adding the lamb meatballs to the pan – depending on the size of the pan, it might be best to cook these in batches to avoid overcrowding. Leave the meatballs to sit and crisp up for 2–3 minutes on all sides, repeating until the meatballs are all crispy and golden brown.
4. Meanwhile, add your rinsed butter beans and 3 tablespoons of Harissa-Tahini Dressing into a bowl and mix together.
5. Thinly slice the radishes and place in a bowl of iced water to crisp up.
6. Thinly slice the preserved lemons, discarding any pips as they appear, but keeping elegant round slices.
7. Place your parsley, coriander and dill onto a chopping board. Remove the bottom 5cm from the stems and discard.
8. Once the lamb meatballs are ready – roughly 10–15 minutes in total – load up your serving plate with most of the herbs, setting some aside for topping the salad. Drizzle with 2 teaspoons of olive oil and a pinch of sea salt. Load on the butter beans, followed by the radishes. Top with the lamb meatballs and dot with slices of preserved lemon. Drizzle with 3 more tablespoons of Harissa-Tahini Dressing and finish with the remaining herbs.

Ingredients
2 tsp cumin seeds
2 tsp coriander seeds
2 tsp fennel seeds
4 tsp sesame seeds
250g lamb mince (20% fat)
¼ tsp fine cooking salt
1 tsp ground cumin
1 tsp cinnamon
2 tbsp + 2 tsp extra virgin olive oil
700g jar of butter beans or 2 x 400g tins of butter beans, drained and rinsed
5 radishes
2 preserved lemons
20g flat leaf parsley
20g fresh coriander
10g dill
5g chives, roughly chopped
Sea salt

READY TO ROCK:

6 tbsp Harissa-Tahini Dressing (see page 172)

TIP:

Finish this with a dollop of garlicky yoghurt and some fresh pitta in place of cutlery to allow you to really get stuck in.

Spicy Cashew Dressing

Dresses 4–6 salads

Spicy Cashew Dressing was one of the first recipes we developed at The Salad Project (after focusing on cracking the perfect Caesar dressing). It's a great dressing to experiment with and really make your own, from altering the viscosity, to working out how toasted you want your cashews. We use it for two plant-based recipes here, but Spicy Cashew works a treat with grilled chicken, roasted salmon, a rare steak and so many other vegetables.

60g whole cashews
90ml water
1 garlic clove
2cm fresh ginger
10g fresh coriander
1 tbsp rice wine vinegar
45ml toasted sesame oil
1 tsp maple syrup
1 lime (juice)
1–2 tsp chilli flakes, plus extra to taste (optional)
1 tsp sea salt, plus extra to taste (optional)

1. Place your cashews into a dry pan over a gentle heat and allow to toast. Keep swirling the pan and don't walk away, to avoid them burning. Add the water to a bowl. Once the cashews reach a golden colour and have a toasty smell, remove them from the heat and place them into the water. Allow to soak for 30 minutes–1 hour.
2. Peel and chop your garlic and ginger. Use the flat side of your knife and a sprinkle of sea salt to crush them together into a garlic-ginger paste.
3. Discard the bottom 5cm from the coriander stems.
4. Place the cashews and their soaking water into a high-speed blender. Add your ginger-garlic paste, coriander leaves and soft stems and all remaining ingredients. Blend for 3–4 minutes until completely smooth.
5. Add extra salt and chilli flakes to taste. Store in an airtight jar or container in the fridge for up to 1 week.

TRY IT WITH:

+ Christina Soteriou's Tofu Knot + Toasted Seed Soba Noodle Salad (see page 125)
+ Thai Me Up (see page 184)
+ Sesame Soy Steak with Furikake Croutons + Pickled Chillies (see page 53)

Kung-Fu Tofu

With Spicy Cashew Dressing

Serves 2   SPICY

+ **Medium-Build**
+ **Protein Power**

This recipe packs a plant-based protein punch, and squeezes in so many different plants with some serious crunch. The final drizzle isn't an afterthought, but a key contributor to the benefits available in the bowl. The only oil used across this salad is a toasted sesame oil, which is loaded with omega-3, omega-6 and omega-9 fats, and is shown to support a reduction in risk of heart disease, a reduction of LDL (bad) cholesterol, and a reduction in inflammation – while boosting serotonin. It's a pretty kick-ass salad.

1. Measure the tamari or soy sauce, maple syrup, 1 tablespoon of the sesame oil and the miso paste into a bowl and whisk well to combine. Drain the tofu and press out as much of the remaining liquid as possible. Chop into 2.5cm cubes. Place the tofu into the marinade, turning the pieces over a couple of times to ensure both sides get coated. Leave to soak for 10–15 minutes.
2. Slice the cucumber in half lengthways and use a teaspoon to scoop out the seeds, then slice into half moons or finely dice. Transfer to a mixing bowl and sprinkle with a pinch of cooking salt and a pinch of caster sugar and set aside.
3. Peel the outer skin off the carrot and discard, then peel the rest of the carrot into broad ribbons and add to the cucumber bowl, along with the rice vinegar. Use your hands to mix.
4. Chop the lettuce chunkily and scatter over a serving plate. Add the spinach, then drizzle in 2 tablespoons of Spicy Cashew Dressing and toss gently to coat. Layer on your carrot and cucumber mix, leaving excess liquid behind.
5. If using frozen edamame beans, cook them in boiling water for 2 minutes, then drain and rinse under cold water to cool. Scatter over the serving plate.
6. Heat 2 tablespoons of the sesame oil in a large frying pan over a medium–high heat. Once hot, add the tofu, leaving behind the excess marinade (you'll use it in a second). Fry until golden on each side, turning the pieces every minute or so for 7 minutes. Once golden, drain the excess oil from the pan, then add the remaining marinade and reduce the heat to medium. As the marinade bubbles, swirl it round the pan until it thickens and starts to caramelise while coating the tofu. Once fully coating the tofu, sprinkle over the furikake seasoning and place the tofu onto your salad.
7. Wipe the residue from the pan and add the cashews. Drizzle with a little sesame oil, sprinkle with sea salt and a couple of grinds of pepper, then toast over a medium heat until golden on all sides. Allow to cool slightly while you drizzle 4 tablespoons of Spicy Cashew Dressing over the assembled salad.
8. Roughly chop the cashews, then sprinkle over the top and complete with a garnish of fresh coriander.

2 tbsp tamari (if making gluten-free) or light soy sauce

2 tbsp maple syrup

3 tbsp toasted sesame oil, plus extra for drizzling

1 tsp white miso paste

250g super-firm tofu

½ cucumber

Pinch of fine cooking salt

Pinch of caster sugar

1 carrot

1 tsp rice vinegar

½–1 cos lettuce, rinsed and dried

Handful of baby spinach

100g edamame beans (fresh or frozen)

2 tsp furikake seasoning

40g whole cashews

Small handful of fresh coriander, leaves picked

Sea salt and black pepper

READY TO ROCK:

6 tbsp Spicy Cashew Dressing (see page 176)

TIP:

Boost the flavour by giving the cucumber a smack. Smack with a rolling pin, scrape out the seeds with a teaspoon and chop into rough chunks. Let it sit in a bowl with a pinch of sea salt and a pinch of sugar. After 10 minutes, dress with 1 teaspoon rice vinegar and 2 teaspoons tamari or light soy sauce. Sprinkle with chilli flakes or crispy chilli oil and add to the salad with the carrots.

Roasted Aubergine, Spicy Cashew Chickpeas + Kale

With Spicy Cashew Dressing

Serves 2

+ Medium-Build
+ Gut Happy

A deliciously filling plant-based Buddha bowl of aubergine, dressed chickpeas and lime-y kale, this salad combines the best of toasty, creamy and fresh flavours. Roll it out in winter or summer to provide a supremely wholesome, but not too heavy, meal that will do what Buddha bowls do best – nourish your mind and body (in just 20 minutes).

1. Preheat the oven to 220°C/200°C fan.
2. Thinly slice the aubergine and place into a large mixing bowl. Add the miso, the soy sauce, the maple syrup, the balsamic vinegar, 1 tablespoon of the sesame oil and the sesame seeds, and use your hands to give the aubergine a good coating. Leave to sit for a couple of minutes to soak up the marinade. Place into a roasting tray and roast in the oven for 20 minutes until dark in colour and slightly crispy.
3. Meanwhile, use the mixing bowl from the aubergine (no need to wash) to massage and dress the kale. Place the kale into the bowl and add 1 teaspoon of the sesame oil, along with the lime zest and juice and the rice vinegar. Use your hands to rub these into the kale for a couple of minutes, then place it onto the serving dish to keep softening.
4. Place the rinsed chickpeas into the same mixing bowl and add 3 tablespoons of Spicy Cashew Dressing.
5. Slice the spring onion from root to tip, then add to the chickpeas, along with a pinch of chilli flakes.
6. Next pour the cashews into a small dry frying pan and place over a medium heat, keeping an eye on the pan to ensure they don't burn. Swirl the nuts around the pan to toast to a golden brown. Add the pinch of sea salt and allow to cool.
7. Dot the sushi ginger in and among the kale, then layer on the dressed chickpeas. Top with the tamari aubergine, then dress the salad with another 3 tablespoons of Spicy Cashew dressing. Finish by scattering over the toasted cashews and, if using, a sprinkling of furikake seasoning. Serve with a wedge of lime.

Ingredients
1 small aubergine
1½ tbsp miso
1½ tbsp soy sauce
1 tbsp maple syrup
1 tsp balsamic vinegar
1 tbsp + 1 tsp toasted sesame oil
2 tsp sesame seeds
2 handfuls of kale, destemmed, rinsed and dried
½ lime (zest and juice), plus lime wedges to serve
1 tsp rice vinegar
570g jar chickpeas (preferably the large Spanish ones) or 2 x 400g tins, drained and rinsed
1 spring onion
Pinch of chilli flakes
80g whole cashews
Pinch of sea salt
2 tbsp sushi ginger
Sprinkle of furikake seasoning (optional)

READY TO ROCK:

6 tbsp Spicy Cashew Dressing (see page 176)

TIP:

This bowl also works great with button or oyster mushrooms subbed in directly for aubergine. Just roast them whole or torn for a juicy alternative – or addition!

SPICY

Thai Peanut Dressing

Dresses 4–6 salads

If you're a peanut butter lover, you'll be whizzing this up on repeat. Luckily, there are so many recipes this dressing works with, so you can keep a jar in your fridge and drizzle it on anything, from plain noodles to honey-soy chicken. If you want to amp up the peanut, opt for a deep roast peanut butter – and please promise to avoid nut butters that list any ingredients other than simply nuts and a little sea salt. Buy only the best for the Thai Peanut and she'll be a life-long fridge friend.

1. Peel the ginger using the edge of a teaspoon, then, using a fine grater or microplane, grate into the blender.
2. Peel and crush your garlic using the side of a knife or a garlic crusher and a little sea salt to help turn it into a smooth paste. Add your garlic paste and all remaining ingredients to a high-speed blender. Blitz to a smooth and silky consistency.
3. Taste, and add more chilli to taste – feel free to really go for it if you'd like more of a kick. Store in an airtight jar or container in the fridge for up to 1 week.

Ingredients
5g fresh ginger
1 garlic clove
90g smooth peanut butter (I'd recommend deep roast)
2 tbsp + 1 tsp rice wine vinegar
1 lime (juice)
2 tbsp sesame oil
2 tbsp tamari or light soy sauce
1½ tbsp maple syrup
1 tbsp water
1 tsp chilli flakes, plus extra to taste (optional)
¼ tsp sea salt

TRY IT WITH:

+ Kung-Fu Tofu (see page 177)
+ Roasted Salmon with Bean Sprouts + Lime Leaf Shred (see page 158)

The Satay Bowl
With Thai Peanut Dressing

Serves 2 SPICY

+ Medium-Build
+ Brain + Body Fuel

We are, indisputably, living in the golden age of beans – which is an absolute gift for the salad-obsessed, because they're the quickest way to add body and flavour to a salad, whether dressed up or dressed down. We partnered with the Bold Bean Co. to launch a grain bowl that put beans under the spotlight. In short, it popped off. Here's the recipe to whip up our nourishing, peanutty chickpea satay bowl at home. PLEASE be sure to use only the best beans – from our friends at Bold Bean Co. if you can get them, or look out for Spanish beans in a jar for a fail-safe alternative.

1. Preheat the oven to 200°C/180°C fan.
2. Place the rice, water and ¼ teaspoon cooking salt into a medium saucepan over a medium–high heat and bring to a boil. Once boiling, reduce the heat and leave to cook and soak up the water for 25 minutes until soft and chewy.
3. Slice the squash into 5mm slices, removing the seeds, but leaving the skin on. Place onto a parchment-lined roasting tray in a single layer and drizzle with 2 teaspoons of the toasted sesame oil, then sprinkle over the sesame seeds. Season with a generous pinch of sea salt. Roast in the oven for 15–20 minutes until soft and just colouring.
4. While that's roasting, take a medium-sized bowl and mix together the peanut butter, miso paste, maple syrup, the juice of 1 lime, chilli flakes or Crispy Chilli Oil, 3 tablespoons of the toasted sesame oil and the reserved chickpea liquid. Use a whisk and keep stirring until it combines into a smooth sauce (it might curdle at the start, but keep going). Finally, fold through the chickpeas and set aside.
5. Slice the roasted red peppers into strands.
6. Slice the cucumber down the middle, then use a teaspoon to scrape out the seeds. Cut down the length of the cucumber in 2cm increments to give you half moons. Put into a bowl with a sprinkle of cooking salt and the caster sugar.
7. When the rice is cooked, fold through the baby spinach and pour onto a serving plate or bowl. Squeeze over the juice of half the remaining lime. Lay over the sesame squash, followed by the sliced peppers, curling the strands into nice shapes. Spoon over the chickpea satay. Strain the cucumber to remove any liquid it's released and scatter over the top, along with the Pickled Chillies. Dress with 3–4 tablespoons of Thai Peanut dressing and finish with the Toasted Furikake Seeds, the coriander leaves and the juice from the remaining half lime.

200g Camargue red rice

500ml water

Fine cooking salt

¼ butternut squash

2 tsp + 3 tbsp toasted sesame oil

1 tbsp sesame seeds

4 tbsp smooth peanut butter

1 tsp white miso paste

2 tsp maple syrup

2 limes (juice)

½ tsp chilli flakes or 1 tbsp Crispy Chilli Oil (see page 31)

570g jar or 400g tin chickpeas (we use Queen Chickpeas from our friends at Bold Bean Co.), drained, 2 tablespoons of liquid reserved

80g roasted red peppers from a jar, drained

½ cucumber

Pinch of caster sugar

Handful of baby spinach

Handful of fresh coriander leaves

Sea salt

READY TO ROCK:

2 tbsp Pickled Chillies (see page 28) or fresh sliced chilli

3–4 tbsp Thai Peanut Dressing (see page 180 – use tamari if gluten-free)

3 tbsp Toasted Furikake Seeds (see page 20) or toasted pumpkin seeds

TIP:

Double the chickpea recipe and keep some of the chickpea satay in the fridge. It's great warmed up with noodles or roasted vegetables and some extra Crispy Chilli Oil.

Thai Me Up
With Thai Peanut Dressing

Serves 2

+ Long-Build
+ Brain + Body Fuel

The Thai Me Up secured a permanent spot in The Salad Project's Hall of Fame when it contributed to our winning the Uber Eats Restaurant of the Year. The Salad Project had been up and running for just over a year, with one site in Spitalfields, when we landed a spot in the final for this event. We created the Thai Me Up salad for our judging panel, which included Prue Leith. Since then, this salad has been a sure-fire favourite for London.

1. Preheat the oven to 220°C/200°C fan.
2. Weigh the pearl barley, water and vegetable stock jelly or cube into a saucepan and bring to a boil over a high heat. Once boiling, reduce the heat and simmer for 30–40 minutes until cooked through. Drain and rinse.
3. Drain the sweetcorn and pour into a roasting tray. Add the olive oil and a generous pinch of sea salt. Stir gently to coat the corn, then place in the oven for 15 minutes.
4. Meanwhile, in a medium mixing bowl, combine the sugar, sriracha, miso paste, tamari or soy sauce, 1 teaspoon of the sesame oil and the juice of half of the lime, stirring until smooth. Add the chicken thighs and mix, ensuring that every crevice is fully coated. Set aside for 10 minutes.
5. When the corn has been roasting for 15 minutes, give it a good stir and return to the oven for a further 15 minutes.
6. While the chicken is marinating, roughly shred the kale and finely shred the cabbage, and place into a bowl. Add 1 teaspoon of the sesame oil, along with the rice vinegar, the juice from the other half of the lime, the sesame seeds, chilli flakes and 2 pinches of sea salt. Massage to soften the kale.
7. Add the corn to the kale and cabbage mix, and use the roasting tray to toast the peanuts. Tip the peanuts onto the tray with a pinch of sea salt and place into the oven for 6–8 minutes until golden and toasted.
8. Dress the cooked and rinsed pearl barley with 1 tablespoon of the sesame oil and the coriander leaves. Place onto a serving plate and top with the kale, cabbage and corn mix. Dress with 2 tablespoons of Thai Peanut Dressing and sprinkle over the toasted peanuts.
9. Heat 1 teaspoon of the sesame oil over a medium–high heat and add the chicken thighs, leaving any excess marinade in the bowl for now. As you place the thighs in the pan, use tongs to flatten them to help them caramelise. Flip them every 30 seconds or so. After 7 minutes, add the remaining marinade and increase the heat to high. Leave the chicken still while the marinade thickens, then turn it over a couple of times. Remove from the pan and place onto a chopping board to rest for a few minutes.
10. Slice the cucumber down the middle and scoop out its seeds using a teaspoon, then slice it into 2cm half moons. Scatter over the salad.
11. Slice the chicken and add it to the dish. Finish with 3–4 tablespoons of Thai Peanut Dressing and the Crispy Chilli Oil or extra peanuts.

100g pearl barley

500ml water

1 vegetable stock jelly or 1 cube

198g tin sweetcorn (in water)

1 tbsp extra virgin olive oil

2 tbsp soft dark brown sugar

1 tsp sriracha

1 tsp white miso paste

1 tbsp tamari or light soy sauce

1 tbsp + 3 tsp toasted sesame oil

1 lime (juice)

4 chicken thighs

Large handful of kale, destemmed, rinsed and dried

⅛ red cabbage

1 tsp rice vinegar

1 tbsp sesame seeds

Pinch of chilli flakes

30g unsalted peanuts

Small handful of fresh coriander leaves

¼ cucumber

Sea salt

READY TO ROCK:

5–6 tbsp Thai Peanut Dressing (see page 180)

2 tbsp Crispy Chilli Oil (see page 31), or just double up on the peanuts listed above

TIP:

Sub the chicken for the Tamari Tofu on page 102 to make this peanutty classic plant-based.

SPICY

Chipotle + Lime Dressing

Dresses 4–6 salads

This dressing was designed especially for this book, and we couldn't stop thinking about it for weeks after first tasting it. Smoky, creamy and zingy, with a touch of sweetness, this dressing transcends the seasons and will elevate your cooking at any time of year. Its warmth serves up the wintery kick we crave on rainy days (drizzle over brown rice or paprika chicken thighs), while its limey zing and touch of maple remind me of tucking into big salads at a barbecue, margarita in hand. A real reminder that salad can be sexy, especially when there are dressings as seductive as this one.

1. Peel and crush your garlic using the side of a knife or a garlic crusher and a little sea salt to help turn it into a smooth paste.
2. Pick the mint leaves from your stems and add, along with all remaining ingredients, into the blender with the garlic. Blend until smooth, then taste and adjust the salt if needed.
3. Finish by stirring through an extra pinch of chipotle chilli flakes to add texture and colour to your dressing. Store in an airtight jar or container in the fridge for up to 1 week.

1 garlic clove

3 stems of mint

110g natural yoghurt or plant-based yoghurt

90g full-fat mayonnaise or plant-based mayonnaise

4 limes (juice)

3 tsp chipotle chilli flakes, plus an extra pinch

1½ tbsp maple syrup

1½ tsp sea salt, plus extra to taste (optional)

TRY IT WITH:

+ Roasted Corn + Red Beans with Crispy Onions + Feta (see page 60)
+ Steak, Sweet Potato + Rocket Salad (see page 138)
+ A Spoonful of Goodness (see page 108)

Sweet and Salty Halloumi, Mango + Mint Salad

With Chipotle + Lime Dressing

Serves 2

+ Quick-Build

It makes my mouth water even thinking about this recipe, which was something I whipped up on one of the hottest days of the year and almost cried with mango-ey, minty joy that these flavours exist. Chill the mango, avocado and mint right down, then take it to the table with some sweet, sticky, salty halloumi right at the last minute. With your jars ready to rock, this will take you 15 minutes to throw together, either for a solo treat to self, a dinner for two (if you can bring yourself to share) or a dinner party platter. The finishing touch here is, of course, a jug of spicy margaritas with a Tajín rim.

1. Place the chopped mango into a bowl with the lime juice and a generous pinch of sea salt.
2. Finely shred the mint leaves with a knife.
3. Lay the seasoned mango onto your serving plate and dot with the Pickled Chillies or fresh chillies.
4. Cut the avocado into chunks of a similar size to the mango and layer onto the plate, scattering half the mint on top. Drizzle over 2 tablespoons of Chipotle + Lime Dressing.
5. Slice the halloumi into 2cm slices. Heat the olive oil in a frying pan over a medium–high heat and, when hot, add your halloumi slices in a single layer. After a couple of minutes, add the honey and chipotle chilli flakes to the pan and swirl. Turn the halloumi using tongs and allow the side facing down to take on some colour for 2–3 minutes before turning back and colouring the first side. Remove from the pan, and lay over the mango and chilli mix.
6. Add the final 2–3 tablespoons of Chipotle + Lime Dressing, then sprinkle over the Toasted Furikake Seeds or toasted pumpkin seeds and some final shreds of mint.

---

2 really ripe mangoes, chopped

½ lime (juice)

Small handful of mint leaves

1 ripe avocado

250g halloumi

2 tbsp extra virgin olive oil

1 tsp runny honey

1 tsp chipotle chilli flakes

Sea salt

READY TO ROCK:

1 tbsp Pickled Chillies (see page 28) or freshly sliced chillies

4–5 tbsp Chipotle + Lime Dressing (see page 186)

2 tbsp Toasted Furikake Seeds (see page 25) or toasted pumpkin seeds

---

TIP:

Whack this mix into some warmed corn tortillas for some fun finger food.

Mex on the Beach

With Chipotle + Lime Dressing

Serves 2

+ Medium-Build

Our co-founder James has always had a soft spot for Mexican food, so this first landed on our menu at his request, celebrating some of the most popular flavours and textures of Mexican cooking. This Tajín-based chicken marinade really tingles on the tongue, and the meat sits atop a salad loaded with elements of spice, sourness, salt and sweetness. It's a really zingy one to whip up after a day that's zapped your energy levels if you want something light and fresh – and if you really need that extra boost, load it up with some brown rice or quinoa and a crumbling of feta. Equally, chop it all up and whack it in a taco. Voilà – Mex on the Beach.

1. Preheat the oven to 220°C/200°C fan.
2. Combine the Tajín, paprika and brown sugar in a medium mixing bowl. Add your chicken breasts and use your hands or tongs to ensure the breasts are fully coated in the dry spice rub.
3. Drain the corn and place into a roasting tray with the olive oil and a generous pinch of sea salt. Mix well to combine. Place both trays into the oven. The chicken will need 20 minutes and the corn will need a first round of 15 minutes.
4. Slice your cos lettuce into chunky pieces, then rinse and dry. Load onto a serving plate.
5. Slice the cucumber in half lengthways and use a teaspoon to scoop out the seeds, then slice crosswise into 1–2cm half moons. Scatter over the cos and dress both with 3 tablespoons of Chipotle + Lime Dressing. Toss to coat.
6. Slice the avocado and distribute the slices across the green base.
7. When its 15 minutes are up, give the corn a mix with a heat-proof spoon or spatula and return to the oven for a further 15 minutes.
8. When its 20 minutes are up, remove the chicken from the tray to allow to rest until the corn is ready.
9. Once the corn is well coloured, sprinkle it with some extra Tajín, then scatter over the dressed leaves, followed by your jalapeños.
10. Slice or shred the chicken and lay on top. Dress with 3 more tablespoons of Chipotle + Lime Dressing, then finish with the crunchy corn, Quick Pickled Onions and the coriander leaves. Squeeze over the lime juice and serve.

---

2 tbsp Tajín seasoning, plus extra for sprinkling

1 tsp smoked paprika

1 tsp soft dark brown sugar

2 chicken breasts

2 x 198g tins sweetcorn (in water)

2 tbsp extra virgin olive oil

½–1 cos lettuce

½ cucumber

1 ripe avocado

2 tbsp jalapeños in brine, drained

4 tbsp crunchy corn (spiced or salted, we use Love Corn)

Small handful of fresh coriander leaves

½ lime (juice)

Sea salt

READY TO ROCK:

6 tbsp Chipotle + Lime Dressing (see page 186)

2 tbsp Quick Pickled Onions (see page 28)

TIP:

For a plant-based option, add 1 tablespoon of sesame oil to marinade a 250g block of tofu, chopped or sliced. Bake in the oven at 200°C/180°C fan for 20 minutes.

Miso-Peanut Dressing

SPICY

Dresses 4–6 salads

Your pocket-rocket dressing that delivers BIG flavour in minutes. There's so much room for play with this miso-based dressing, from dialling up the spice with sriracha, to piling on the peanut butter if that's more your style. In its classic, gingery form, we love it as a fridge staple thanks to its power to pull any random assortment of fresh ingredients hiding in your vegetable drawers into something to be proud of. It's the perfect partner to boost so many dishes, from grilled salmon, trout or tuna to chicken thighs, tofu or roasted vegetables.

45g fresh ginger

75g white miso paste

3 limes (juice), plus extra to taste (optional)

40g smooth peanut butter

40g sriracha, plus extra to taste (optional)

110ml toasted sesame oil

1. Peel the ginger using the edge of a teaspoon and grate, using a microplane or fine grater, into a blender.
2. Add the remaining ingredients and blend until silky smooth.
3. Taste and adjust the lime juice or sriracha to taste. Store in an airtight jar or container in the fridge for up to 1 week.

TRY IT WITH:

+ Christina Soteriou's Tofu Knot + Toasted Seed Soba Noodle Salad (see page 125)
+ Thai Me Up (see page 184)

Icy, Spicy Noodles + Silken Tofu

With Miso-Peanut Dressing

Serves 2

+ Quick-Build
+ Protein Power

A salad built out of utter desperation (as all the best salads are), when London was melting under the summer sun. You know what they say, if you can't handle the heat, get out of the kitchen – and this recipe will get you out of there pronto, because it takes as long as it takes to refresh ready-to-eat noodles and chop a cucumber. Just make sure you have ice at the ready, because this is best served COLD.

1. Place the noodles into a heat-proof bowl and boil the kettle. Make sure your silken tofu is in the fridge to keep it cold until the last minute.
2. Once the water is boiling, pour over the noodles to cover and leave for 3 minutes. Drain and place the noodles back into the bowl, with 4 ice cubes and enough cold water to cover the noodles. Add the sugar snap peas to crisp up. Set aside.
3. Place the Miso-Peanut Dressing in a bowl and add 1 ice cube. Let it sit to chill and loosen.
4. Dice your cucumber into small pieces and place in a bowl with the salt, caster sugar and chilli flakes to draw out some moisture.
5. Drain the ice noodles and sugar snaps, then return to the bowl.
6. Give the ice cube in the dressing a stir around the dressing so the water released blends into it, then remove and discard the ice cube. Add 4 tablespoons of the iced dressing to the bowl of noodles and sugar snaps. Use tongs to swirl the dressing evenly through the noodles and sugar snaps. Lay the dressed noodles onto a serving plate and top with the whole coriander stems.
7. Strain off any liquid from the cucumber, then sprinkle the cucumber over the coriander.
8. Use scissors to open the fridge-cold tofu, drain, and gently place it on top of the noodle bed. Dress the tofu with the remaining chilled dressing, then top with the tamari or soy sauce and rice vinegar. Drizzle the Crispy Chilli Oil over the dish.
9. Finely slice your spring onions at an angle and sprinkle over the salad, followed by the coriander leaves for garnish. Finish with an extra sprinkle of chilli flakes to add a little extra heat. Serve immediately!

400g ready-to-eat udon noodles

250g silken tofu, well chilled

5 large ice cubes

100g sugar snap peas

½ cucumber

Pinch of fine cooking salt

Pinch of caster sugar

Pinch of chilli flakes, plus a little extra to garnish

Handful of fresh coriander, stems intact, plus leaves to garnish

2 tbsp tamari or light soy sauce

1 tsp rice vinegar

2 spring onions

READY TO ROCK:

8 tbsp Miso-Peanut Dressing (see page 190)

3 tbsp Crispy Chilli Oil (see page 31)

TIP:

As a quick substitute for Crispy Chilli Oil, mix together 2 tablespoons tamari, 1 teaspoon caster sugar, 1 teaspoon sesame oil, 2 teaspoon sesame seeds, ½ teaspoon chilli flakes, 2 crushed garlic cloves, ½ red chilli, finely chopped, and a spring onion.

Miso Salmon
With Miso-Peanut Dressing

Serves 2

SPICY

+ **Medium-Build**
+ **Protein Power**

Red rice, greens and salmon: this is your go-to if you're in need of some nourishment after a long day at work or a session in the gym. With the perfect balance of slow-releasing carbohydrates, lean protein and the best brain-fuelling fats you can find, this should be the bowl you return to time and time again to help reset your body's balance. There's a reason it's been a long-standing favourite at The Salad Project and, put simply, it's because it's built to make you feel *good*.

1. Preheat the oven to 220°C/200°C fan, and line a large roasting tray with parchment paper.
2. Place the rice, water and cooking salt into a medium saucepan over a medium–high heat and bring to a boil. Once boiling, reduce the heat and leave to cook and soak up the water for 25 minutes until soft and chewy.
3. Place the salmon fillets in the centre of the lined tray and spread 1 tablespoon of Miso-Peanut Dressing over each fillet. Lay the broccoli around the salmon and drizzle with the olive oil and a pinch of sea salt. Roast for 12 minutes.
4. Meanwhile, cook the edamame, if frozen, by boiling some water in a saucepan, adding the beans and cooking for 2 minutes before draining and chilling under running cold water, or in a bowl of iced water.
5. When the rice, salmon and broccoli are ready, toss the rice and spinach together in a bowl and dress with 2 tablespoons of Miso-Peanut Dressing. Pile onto the serving plate. Sprinkle over the edamame and toss in the Toasted Furikake Seeds or toasted sesame seeds. Evenly distribute the sushi ginger over the top.
6. Cut the avocado into nice chunks and scatter evenly over the top.
7. Squeeze the juice of half the lime over the avocado, then layer on the roasted broccoli and finally the salmon. Top the salmon with the Crispy Chilli Oil and dress the salad with another 2 tablespoons of Miso-Peanut Dressing. Garnish with the coriander leaves and finish by squeezing over the second half of the lime.

200g Camargue red rice

500ml water

¼ tsp fine cooking salt

2 salmon fillets

150g Tenderstem broccoli

1 tsp extra virgin olive oil

100g edamame beans (fresh or frozen)

2 handfuls of baby spinach

2 tbsp pickled sushi ginger

1 ripe avocado

1 lime (juice)

Handful of fresh coriander leaves

Sea salt

READY TO ROCK:

5 tbsp Miso-Peanut Dressing (see page 190)

2 tsp Toasted Furikake Seeds (see page 25) or toasted sesame seeds

3 tbsp Crispy Chilli Oil (see page 31) or toasted cashews

TIP:

Sub the salmon for a jammy boiled egg, or find yourself some sashimi-grade salmon from your fishmonger to turn this into a delicious poke bowl.

SPICY

SP's Hot Sauce

One of the longest-serving members of The Salad Project's dressing line-up and, in our opinion, a bit of an unsung hero. This dressing will last at least two weeks in the fridge, and provides a great base to tone up or tone down to your signature spice level. So, if you like to collect bottles of half-used hot sauce in your fridge, here's your answer to an easily accessible boost in heat, healthy nutrients and storage space. Excellent with fried chicken, if we're allowed to say that in a salad book.

1. Add all the ingredients into a blender. Blitz until smooth.
2. Taste and adjust the heat level to your liking by adding some extra cayenne or paprika. Store in an airtight jar or container in the fridge for up to 2 weeks.

| 70g roasted red peppers from a jar, drained |
| 2 limes (juice) |
| 20ml apple cider vinegar |
| 1 tbsp caster sugar |
| 70ml extra virgin olive oil |
| 2 tsp smoked paprika, plus extra to taste (optional) |
| 2 tsp cayenne pepper, plus extra to taste (optional) |
| 1 tsp sea salt |

TRY IT WITH:

+ Any dishes that need a fresh and zingy kick!

Weekly Menus 195-199

Fuel Fitness – Three dressings and five salads that prioritise protein and complex carbohydrates to pre-fuel or refuel you around your weekly workout routine in order to keep you performing at, and feeling, your best.

Keep it Quick – A selection of quick-build salads for the busier weeks when being tight on time doesn't need to mean being tight on nutrition.

Boost the Brain – Salads and grain bowls designed to supercharge your body and mind, from whole grains that help ward off brain fog to omega-3 filled seeds, nuts and oily fish to optimise cognitive function.

Go with Your Gut – Heaps of whole grains, polyphenols and prebiotic-rich ferments to keep your gut's microbiome (and ultimately you) happy.

WEEKLY MENUS

	Sunday	Monday	Tuesday
Prep or In Stock	Miso-Peanut Dressing (see page 190) Real-Deal Green Goddess (see page 146) Toasted Furikake Seeds (see page 25)		
Salad		Miso Salmon (see page 193)	Honey Chicken + Jalapeño Quinoa Salad with Toasted Pine Nuts + Tenderstem (see page 148)

	Sunday	Monday	Tuesday
Prep or In Stock	Whipped Feta + Dill Drizzle (see page 62) Sesa-Miso Dressing (see page 52) Pickled Chillies (see page 28) Toasted Furikake Seeds (see page 25)		
Salad		Beetroot + Chorizo with Hot Honey + Toasted Buckwheat (see page 65)	Chilled Sesame Noodles with Balsamic Mushrooms, Lime Slaw + Toasted Furikake Seeds (see page 57)

Fuel Fitness

Wednesday	Thursday	Friday	Saturday
			Ballymaloe's French Dressing **(see page 104)**
Icy, Spicy Noodles with Silken Tofu **(see page 191)**	Green-Godd-Eggs-on-Toast **(see page 150)**	Leftovers	Tuna Steak Niçoise + Jammy Eggs **(see page 106)**

Keep it Quick

Wednesday	Thursday	Friday	Saturday
			Coconut Ranch Dressing **(see page 58)**
Tomatoes on Toast with Minty Courgette Ribbons + Capers **(see page 66)**	Leftovers	Sesame Soy Steak with Furikake Croutons + Pickled Chillies **(see page 53)**	Roasted Corn + Red Beans with Crispy Onions + Feta **(see page 60)**

WEEKLY MENUS

	Sunday	Monday	Tuesday
Prep or In Stock	Thai Peanut Dressing (see page 180) Coconutty-Curry + Lime Dressing (see page 42) Quick Pickled Onions (see page 28) Crispy Chilli Oil (see page 31)		
Salad		Thai Me Up (see page 184)	God Save the Bean (see page 44)

	Sunday	Monday	Tuesday
Prep or In Stock	Gochujang, Coconut + Ginger Dressing (see page 156) Green Tahini Dressing (see page 124) Crispy Chilli Oil (see page 31)		
Salad		Cold Soba Noodles with Kimchi, Pickled Cucumbers + Sesame Tenderstem (see page 157)	Crispy Mushroom + Smacked Cucumber Rice Bowl (see page 129)

Boost the Brain

Wednesday	Thursday	Friday	Saturday
Caper + Dill Dressing **(see page 130)**			
Icy, Spicy Noodles with Silken Tofu **(see page 191)**		The Satay Bowl **(see page 181)**	Curry-Mango Chicken with Lime Leaf Brown Rice **(see page 43)**

Go with Your Gut

Wednesday	Thursday	Friday	Saturday
			Preserved Lemon + Sour Cream Dressing **(see page 98)** Quick Pickled Onions **(see page 28)**
Leftovers	Roasted Salmon with Bean Sprouts + Lime Leaf Shred **(see page 158)**	Christina Soteriou's Tofu Knot + Toasted Seed Soba Noodle Salad **(see page 125)**	Crispy Spiced Lamb, Aubergine + Freekeh with Pickled Onions **(see page 100)**

SP Cookie

Bonus Recipe

Makes 12–14

We're big proponents of living a balanced life and so, as a thank you for wading through 56 salad recipes, it's only fair we lift the lid on the SP Cookie recipe. You're welcome.

1. Using a stand mixer, or a wooden spoon and a large bowl, cream the softened butter and two sugars together until light and fluffy (about 5 minutes). Add the egg and beat until very well combined.
2. Weigh the dry ingredients, excluding the sea salt, into a separate bowl and whisk to combine.
3. Add the dry ingredients to the wet mixture and mix in as quickly as you are able without over mixing. Fold in the chocolate until evenly dispersed.
4. Using your hands, roll the dough into 70g balls and place in a parchment-lined container. Place in the fridge for at least 3 hours. In the fridge, the cookie dough will keep for 4 days; in the freezer, it will keep for 2 weeks.
5. On the day of baking, preheat the oven to 180°C/160°C fan.
6. Lay the dough balls onto a lined baking sheet, with plenty of space around each cookie to allow it to spread while baking. Cook for 12 minutes (14 minutes if the dough came from the freezer), then remove from the oven and sprinkle each cookie with a pinch of sea salt while still warm. Allow to cool – or devour warm.

175g salted butter, softened

175g soft dark brown sugar

140g caster sugar

1 large egg

¾ tsp baking powder

1 tsp bicarbonate of soda

315g plain flour

150g dark chocolate (or large chocolate buttons), chopped into small chunks

Sea salt

Index

Note: page numbers in bold refer to illustrations

A
acids **10**, 10, 13–14, 17
almond(s)
  smoky toasted almonds **94**, 95
  sweet + smoky paprika almonds 25, **26**, 80, 95, 96
apple cider vinaigrette 8, 76, 77, 80
aubergine
  crispy spiced lamb, aubergine + freekeh with pickled onions 100, **101**
  roasted aubergine, spicy cashew chickpeas + kale 178, **179**
  roasted aubergine with quinoa, maple walnuts + pomegranate 49, **51**
avocado 38, 44, 59–60, 80, 95, 108, 129, 146, 187–8, 193

B
bacon 168
  potato salad with smoked bacon + shredded roast chicken 59
balsamic mushrooms **56**, 57
bases 11, **11**
basil 58, 89, 108, 118, 122, 136, 144, 146, 148
batch prepping 18
bean(s) 53–4, 106
  God save the bean 44, **45**
  roasted corn + red beans with crispy onions + feta 60, **61**
  see also butter bean(s); edamame bean(s)
beetroot 84
  beetroot + chorizo with hot honey + toasted buckwheat **64**, 65
blue cheese, salty-and-sweet cavolo nero, quinoa + black cherry salad with blue cheese + maple walnuts **170**, 171
brown butter + miso vinaigrette 110, 111, 113
buckwheat
  toasted **64**, 65
  toasted maple **112**, 113
bulgur wheat 69, 96, 100
burrata 113, 144
  burrata + spring 137
  roasted courgette + burrata with chickpeas + garlicky seeds 90, **91**
butter bean(s) 144
  garlic + thyme chicken, butter bean + sun-dried tomato 89
  God save the bean 44, **45**
  whole-spice lamb meatballs, preserved lemon + butter bean salad 174, **175**

C
cabbage
  cabbage slaw 102, **103**
  shredded cabbage with garlic-thyme chicken thighs + pomegranate seeds 168, 169
  see also red cabbage
Caesar dressing 8, 32
  see also chipotle Caesar dressing
capers 12, 106, 134, 136
  caper + dill dressing 130, **131**, 133–4
  tomatoes on toast with minty courgette ribbons + capers 66, **67**
carrot 168, 171, 177
  honey carrots 69
cashew nut 13, 177
  spicy cashew chickpeas 178, **179**
  spicy cashew dressing 176–8
cauliflower, spiced cauliflower with smoky toasted almonds + hot honey labneh **94**, 95
cavolo nero, salty-and-sweet cavolo nero, quinoa + black cherry salad with blue cheese + maple walnuts **170**, 171
cheese see burrata; feta; goat's cheese; halloumi; Parmesan
cherry, salty-and-sweet cavolo nero, quinoa + black cherry salad **170**, 171
chicken
  chicken Thai me up **183**, 184
  curry mango chicken with lime leaf brown rice 43
  garlic + thyme chicken, butter bean + sun-dried tomato 89
  the GOAT 119–20
  honey chicken + jalapeño quinoa salad with toasted pine nuts + Tenderstem 148, **149**
  the market bowl 84
  Mex on the beach 188, **189**
  miso chicken with crispy spiced chickpeas + pickled cucumbers 48, **50**
  the Octoberfest: maple chicken + chorizo grain bowl 111
  paprika chicken thigh with nutty grains + roasted peppers 96, **97**
  potato salad with smoked bacon + shredded roast chicken 59
  shredded cabbage with garlic-thyme chicken thighs + pomegranate seeds 168, **169**
  SP Caesar salad 41
chickpea(s) 90, 91, 129, 181
  crispy spiced chickpeas 48, **50**
  spicy cashew chickpeas 178, **179**
chilli see crispy chilli oil; pickled chillies
chipotle
  chipotle + lime dressing 186–8
  chipotle Caesar dressing 36, **37**, 38, 41
chorizo
  beetroot + chorizo with hot honey + toasted buckwheat **64**, 65
  the Octoberfest: maple chicken + chorizo grain bowl 111
coconut milk 13
coconutty-curry + lime dressing 42
gochujang, coconut + ginger dressing 156–8
coconut yoghurt 13, 42, 44, 156–8
coconut ranch dressing 58
cookie, SP 200, **201**
coriander (fresh) 42–3, 53–4, 57, 60, 124–6, 146, 156–7, 163, 173–4, 176–7, 181, 184, 188, 191, 193
courgette 122, 143
  minty courgette ribbons 66, **67**
  roasted courgette + burrata with chickpeas + garlicky seeds 90, **91**

INDEX

couscous 65, 111
  harissa steak + giant couscous with pickled onions + pistachios 70, **71**
crispy chilli oil **26**, 31
  recipes using 43, 125–6, 129, 184, 191
crispy onions 24, **26–7**
  recipes using 38, 41, 60, **61**, 102, **103**, 134, 138, 158, 193
cucumber 43, 49, 86, 95, 108, 134, 163, 177, 181, 184, 188, 191
  crispy mushroom + smacked cucumber rice bowl **128**, 129
  pickled cucumbers 48, **50**, 157
curry 44
  coconutty-curry + lime dressing 42
  curry mango chicken with lime leaf brown rice 43

D

date molasses 14
  spiced tahini + date molasses dressing 46, **47**, 48, 49
dill 58, 65, 95, 157, 174
  caper + dill dressing 130, **131**, 133–4
  hot honey halloumi + dill fatoush 86, **87**
  whipped feta + dill drizzle 62, **63**, 65, 66
dressings 8–10, 18
  Ballymaloe's French 104, **105**, 106, **107**, 108
  caper + dill 130, **131**, 133–4
  chipotle + lime 186–8
  chipotle Caesar 36, **37**, 38, 41
  coconut ranch 58, 59, 60
  coconutty-curry + lime 42, 43, 44
  formula 10, **10**
  fresh mint drizzle 140, **141**, 143–4
  gochujang, coconut + ginger 156–8
  green tahini 124–6, 129
  harissa-tahini 172–4
  miso-mustard 166, **167**, 168, 171
  miso-peanut 190, 191, 193
  preserved lemon + sour cream 98, **99**, 100, 102
  real-deal green goddess 146, **147**, 148, 150

romesco drizzle 92, **93**, 95–6
salad formula 11, **11**
salsa verde 136–8
sesa-miso 52, **53–4**, 57
the SP green goddess 118–20, **121**, 122
spiced tahini + date molasses 46, **47**, 48, 49
spicy cashew 176–8
SP's hot sauce 194
tahini + preserved lemon 68–70
Thai peanut 180–1, 184
whipped feta + dill drizzle 62, **63**, 65, 66
see also vinaigrettes

E

edamame bean(s) 77, 80, 158, 177, 192
egg(s) 122, 129, 200
  green godd-eggs-on-toast 150, **151**
  jammy eggs 106, **107**

F

fatoush, hot honey halloumi + dill 86, **87**
fats 10, **10**, 13, 17
feta 12, 44, 49, 108
  roasted corn + red beans with crispy onions + feta 60, **61**
  whipped feta + dill drizzle 62, **63**, 65, 66
freekeh, crispy spiced lamb, aubergine + freekeh with pickled onions 100, **101**
French dressing, Ballymaloe's 104, **105**, 106, **107**, 108
furikake seasoning 177, 178
  furikake croutons 53–4, **55**
see also toasted furikake seeds

G

garlic
  garlic + thyme chicken 89, 168, **169**
  garlicky seeds 90, **91**
ginger, gochujang, coconut + ginger dressing 156–8
goat's cheese 80, 84, 119–20
gochujang, coconut + ginger

dressing 156–8
grains
  lemony 69
  nutty 96, **97**
  Octoberfest grain bowl 111

H

halloumi
  hot honey halloumi + dill fatoush 86, **87**
  sweet and salty halloumi, mango + mint salad 187
harissa 70, 95
  curly 'n' cold harissa noodles with sesame squash 173
  harissa steak + giant couscous with pickled onions + pistachios 70, **71**
  harissa-tahini dressing 172–4
herbs 17
honey 14
  honey carrots 69
  honey chicken + jalapeño quinoa salad with toasted pine nuts + Tenderstem 148, **149**
  see also hot honey
hot honey **27**, 31
  recipes using **64**, 65, 86, **87**, **94**, 95
hot sauce, SP's 194

J

jalapeños 148, **149**, 188

K

kale 38, 41, 84, 111, 184
  roasted aubergine, spicy cashew chickpeas + kale 178, **179**
kimchi 57, 125–6
  cold soba noodles with kimchi, pickled cucumbers + sesame Tenderstem 157

L

labneh, hot honey **94**, 95
lamb
  crispy spiced lamb, aubergine + freekeh with pickled onions 100, **101**
  whole-spice lamb meatballs, preserved lemon + butter bean salad 174, **175**

203

INDEX

lamb's lettuce (mâche) 89, 100, 137
lemon 14
  lemon + thyme vinaigrette 88–90
  lemony grains 69
lemon (preserved) 12
  preserved lemon + sour cream dressing 98, **99**, 100, 102
  tahini + preserved lemon dressing 68–70
  whole-spice lamb meatballs, preserved lemon + butter bean salad 174, **175**
lettuce 148
  baby gem 31, 43, 48, 150, 163
  cos 77, 106, 177, 188
lime 14
  chipotle + lime dressing 186–8
  coconutty-curry + lime dressing 42, 43, 44
  lime slaw **56**, 57
  pomegranate + lime vinaigrette 82, **83**, 84, 86
lime leaf
  lime leaf brown rice 43
  lime leaf shred 158, **159**

M

mango 44
  curry mango chicken with lime leaf brown rice 43
  prawn + mango salad 164, **165**
  sweet and salty halloumi, mango + mint salad 187
maple walnuts 24, **26–7**
  recipes using 49, **51**, 111, 119–20, 144, 168, **170**, 171
mayonnaise 13, 36, 58, 98, 134, 186
meatballs, whole-spice lamb meatballs, preserved lemon + butter bean salad 174, **175**
menu planning 19, 195–9
mint 108, 118, 122, 137, 144, 146, 164, 173
  fresh mint drizzle 140, **141**, 143–4
  green 'n' minty whole grain pasta salad **142**, 143
  minty courgette ribbons 66, **67**
  sweet and salty halloumi, mango + mint salad 187
miso
  miso salmon 192, 193
  see also white miso paste
mushroom
  balsamic mushrooms **56**, 57
  crispy mushroom + smacked cucumber rice bowl **128**, 129
mustard, miso-mustard dressing 166, **167**, 168, 171

N

Niçoise, tuna steak Niçoise + jammy eggs 106, **107**
noodles
  aromatic pork larb + noodle salad with toasted peanuts **162**, 163
  chilled sesame noodles with balsamic mushrooms, lime slaw + toasted furikake seeds **56**, 57
  Christina Soteriou's tofu knot + toasted seed soba noodle salad 125–6, **127**
  cold soba noodles with kimchi, pickled cucumbers + sesame Tenderstem 157
  curly 'n' cold harissa noodles with sesame squash 173
  icy, spicy noodles + silken tofu 191
  tamari tofu with vermicelli noodles, cabbage slaw + crispy onions 102, **103**
nutty grains 96, **97**

O

oils 13
  see also crispy chilli oil
onion *see* crispy onions; quick pickled onions

P

paprika
  paprika chicken thigh 96, **97**
  sweet + smoky paprika almonds 25, **26**, 80, 95, 96
Parmesan 12, 36, 38, 41, 89, 122, 138, 148
parsley (flat leaf) 44, 58, 70, 86, 95, 96, 98, 100, 102, 108, 136, 174
pasta, green 'n' minty whole grain pasta salad **142**, 143
pea shoot(s) 53–4, 70, 158
peaches + cream 144, **145**
peanut 31, 129, 184
  toasted **162**, 163
peanut butter 13, 156, 181
  miso-peanut dressing 190, **191**, 193
  Thai peanut dressing 180–1, 184
pepper (roasted red bell) 92, 96, **97**, 181, 194
pickles
  pickled chillies **27**, 28, **29**, 53–4, 60, 77, 163, 181, 187
  pickled cucumbers 48, **50**, 157
  pickled radish **132**, 133
  see also quick pickled onions
pine nut 122, 133, 148, **149**
pistachio 44, 70, **71**
pomegranate molasses 14
pomegranate + lime vinaigrette 82, **83**, 84, 86
pomegranate seed 49, **51**, 69, 96, 168, **169**
pork
  aromatic pork larb + noodle salad with toasted peanuts **162**, 163
  pork mì 77, **78–9**
potato 106, 134
  Clem's potato salad 122, **123**
  crispy new potatoes, whipped ricotta + pickled radish **132**, 133
  potato salad with smoked bacon + shredded roast chicken 59
prawn
  prawn + mango salad with roasted sweet potatoes 164, **165**
  prawn star salad 38, **39**
pumpkin seed
  garlicky seeds 90, **91**
  see also toasted furikake seeds

Q

quick pickled onions **27**, 28, **29**
  recipes using 43, 70, **71**, 86, 100, **101**, 111, 119–20, 150, 164, 188
quinoa 108
  honey chicken + jalapeño quinoa salad 148, **149**
  roasted aubergine with quinoa, maple walnuts + pomegranate 49, **51**
  salty-and-sweet cavolo nero, quinoa + black cherry salad **170**, 171

R

radicchio 49, 90, 100
radish 53–4, 86, 122, 129, 137, 174
   pickled radish **132**, 133
ranch dressing *see* coconut ranch dressing
red cabbage 77, 111, 158, 184
   cabbage slaw 102, **103**
   lime slaw 57
rice 53–4, 84, 181, 193
   crispy mushroom + smacked cucumber rice bowl **128**, 129
   lime leaf brown rice 43
ricotta, whipped **132**, 133
rocket 52–3, 66, 70, 80, 96, 113, 119–20, 122, 134, 137, 143–4
   steak, sweet potato + rocket salad 138, **139**
romesco drizzle dressing 92, **93**, 95–6

S

salads
   aromatic pork larb + noodle salad with toasted peanuts **162**, 163
   beetroot + chorizo with hot honey + toasted buckwheat **64**, 65
   burrata + spring 137
   chilled sesame noodles with balsamic mushrooms, lime slaw + toasted furikake seeds **56**, 57
   Christina Soteriou's tofu knot + toasted seed soba noodle salad 125–6, **127**
   Clem's potato salad 122, **123**
   cold soba noodles with kimchi, pickled cucumbers + sesame Tenderstem 157
   crispy mushroom + smacked cucumber rice bowl **128**, 129
   crispy new potatoes, whipped ricotta + pickled radish **132**, 133
   crispy spiced lamb, aubergine + freekeh with pickled onions 100, **101**
   curly 'n' cold harissa noodles with sesame squash 173
   curry mango chicken with lime leaf brown rice 43
   formula 11, **11**
   garlic + thyme chicken, butter bean + sun-dried tomato 89
   the GOAT 119–20, **121**
   God save the bean 44, **45**
   green + crunch 80, **81**
   green godd-eggs-on-toast 150, **151**
   green 'n' minty whole grain pasta salad **142**, 143
   harissa steak + giant couscous with pickled onions + pistachios 70, **71**
   honey chicken + jalapeño quinoa salad with toasted pine nuts + Tenderstem 148, **149**
   hot honey halloumi + dill fatoush 86, **87**
   icy, spicy noodles + silken tofu 191
   kung-fu tofu 177
   the market bowl 84, **85**
   Mex on the beach 188, **189**
   miso chicken with crispy spiced chickpeas + pickled cucumbers 48, **50**
   miso salmon **192**, 193
   the Octoberfest: maple chicken + chorizo grain bowl 111
   paprika chicken thigh with nutty grains + roasted peppers 96, **97**
   peaches + cream 144, **145**
   pork mì 77, **78–9**
   potato salad with smoked bacon + shredded roast chicken 59
   prawn + mango salad with roasted sweet potatoes **164**, 165
   the prawn star 38, **39**
   roasted aubergine, spicy cashew chickpeas + kale 178, **179**
   roasted aubergine with quinoa, maple walnuts + pomegranate 49, **51**
   roasted corn + red beans with crispy onions + feta 60, **61**
   roasted courgette + burrata with chickpeas + garlicky seeds 90, **91**
   roasted salmon with bean sprouts + lime leaf shred 158, **159**
   roasted squash, stracciatella + toasted maple buckwheat **112**, 113
   salty-and-sweet cavolo nero, quinoa + black cherry salad with blue cheese + maple walnuts **170**, 171
   the satay bowl 181, **182**
   sesame soy steak with furikake croutons + pickled chillies 53–4, **55**
   shredded cabbage with garlic-thyme chicken thighs + pomegranate seeds 168, **169**
   the SP Caesar salad **40**, 41
   spiced cauliflower with smoky toasted almonds + hot honey labneh **94**, 95
   a spoonful of goodness 108, **109**
   the spring fling 134, **135**
   steak, sweet potato + rocket salad 138, **139**
   sumac salmon with honey carrots, roasted Tenderstem + lemony grains 69
   sweet and salty halloumi, mango + mint salad 187
   tamari tofu with vermicelli noodles, cabbage slaw + crispy onions 102, **103**
   Thai me up **183**, 184
   tomatoes on toast with minty courgette ribbons + capers 66, **67**
   tuna steak Niçoise + jammy eggs 106, **107**
   whole-spice lamb meatballs, preserved lemon + butter bean salad 174, **175**
salmon
   miso salmon **192**, 193
   roasted salmon with bean sprouts + lime leaf shred 158, **159**
   the spring fling 134
   sumac salmon with honey carrots, roasted Tenderstem + lemony grains 69
salsa verde 136–8
salt 10, **10**, 12, 17
satay bowl, the 181, **182**
seed(s)

INDEX

garlicky seeds 90, **91**
toasted seeds 125–6, **127**
see also specific seeds; toasted furikake seeds
sesa-miso dressing 52, 53–4, 57
sesame oil, toasted 13
  sesame soy steak with furikake croutons + pickled chillies 53–4, **55**
sesame seed 31, 48, 102, 158, 174, 178, 181
  chilled sesame noodles with balsamic mushrooms, lime slaw + toasted furikake seeds **56**, 57
  sesa-miso dressing 52
  sesame squash 173
  sesame Tenderstem 157
slaw
  cabbage 102, **103**
  lime **56**, 57
sour cream 13
  preserved lemon + sour cream dressing 98, **99**, 100, 102
sourdough
  furikake croutons 53–4, **55**
  green godd-eggs-on-toast 150, **151**
  tomatoes on toast with minty courgette ribbons + capers 66, **67**
spices 17
spinach (baby) 44, 118, 125–6, 129, 134, 177, 181, 193
squash, roasted squash, stracciatella + toasted maple buckwheat **112**, 113
steak
  harissa steak + giant couscous with pickled onions + pistachios 70, **71**
  sesame soy steak with furikake croutons + pickled chillies 53–4, **55**
  steak, sweet potato + rocket salad 138, **139**
  tuna steak Niçoise + jammy eggs 106, **107**
stracciatella, roasted squash, stracciatella + toasted maple buckwheat **112**, 113

sugar snap pea(s) 43, 108, 158, 191
sugars 14
sumac salmon with honey carrots, roasted Tenderstem + lemony grains 69
sunflower seed
  garlicky seeds 90, **91**
  see also toasted furikake seeds
sweet flavours 10, **10**, 14, 17
sweet potato 84, 119–20
  roasted sweet potatoes 164, **165**
  steak, sweet potato + rocket salad 138, **139**
sweetcorn 38, 184, 188
  roasted corn + red beans with crispy onions + feta 60, **61**

T

tahini 13, 52
  green tahini dressing 124–6, 129
  harissa-tahini dressing 172–4
  spiced tahini + date molasses dressing 46, **47**, 48, 49
  tahini + preserved lemon dressing 68–70
Tajín seasoning 60, 153, 187–8
tamari 12
  tamari tofu with vermicelli noodles, cabbage slaw + crispy onions 102, **103**
Tenderstem broccoli 80, 125–6, 133, 148, **149**, 193
  roasted Tenderstem 69
  sesame Tenderstem 157
thyme
  garlic + thyme chicken 89, 168, **169**
  lemon + thyme vinaigrette 88–90
toast
  green godd-eggs-on-toast 150, 151
  tomatoes on toast with minty courgette ribbons + capers 66, **67**
toasted furikake seeds 25, 57
  recipes using 77, 80, 108, 137, 143, 150, 181, 187, 193
tofu
  Christina Soteriou's tofu knot + toasted seed soba noodle salad 125–6, **127**
  icy, spicy noodles + silken tofu 191

kung-fu tofu 177
  tamari tofu with vermicelli noodles, cabbage slaw + crispy onions 102, **103**
tomato (cherry) 41, 86, 106, 119–20, 138, 143
  tomatoes on toast with minty courgette ribbons + capers 66, **67**
tomato (sun-dried) 122
  garlic + thyme chicken, butter bean + sun-dried tomato 89
toppings 11, **11**
tuna steak Niçoise + jammy eggs 106, **107**

V

vinaigrette 75
  apple cider 76, 77, 80
  brown butter + miso 110, 111, 113
  lemon + thyme 88–90
  pomegranate + lime 82, **83**, 84, 86
  Thai 160, **161**, 163–4
vinegars 13–14

W

walnut *see* maple walnuts
watercress 53–4, 95, 134
white miso paste 12
  brown butter + miso vinaigrette 110, 111, 113
  miso chicken with crispy spiced chickpeas + pickled cucumbers 48, **50**
  miso-mustard dressing 166, **167**, 168, 171
  miso-peanut dressing 190, 191, 193
  sesa-miso dressing 52, 53–4, 57

Y

yoghurt (natural) 13, 95, 140, 146, 186

Thank Yous

This book, and The Salad Project itself, are the result of the work of many hands.

Thank you, first and foremost, to James and Flo, for entrusting me with putting The Salad Project onto paper. You envisaged my ability to create this book long before I imagined it possible, and keep me inspired by dreaming big for The Salad Project. We march on, and it's always a blast.

Thank you to our teams who patiently put up with me using your kitchen space during mad summer lunch services to test recipes and for bringing many of these recipes to life every day across our stores with your hard work and energy.

Thank you to our HQ team for letting my focus be split over the summer of writing this book. Specifically, to our marketing rockstar, Courtenay Lewis, for keeping our marketing ship sailing so smoothly while I squirrelled away in the kitchen multiple days a week.

Thank you to my immense friends, for so many things. For sustaining excitement as I sent you 20, 50, 100 pages of recipes to test and feedback on with a Google Form, and for actually testing them (!). For bearing with me as this project took up three months of weekends and weeknights. For keeping me going with your unwavering support and reminding me it's just salad. I am so grateful for you.

Thank you to Leo for eating more salad than any sane person should in the space of a month, and to baby Joey for your invaluable feedback.

Thank you to my epic family, and in particular my Mum, Viv, for being a better hype crew than I could possibly deserve.

Thank you to the kind, patient and supportive team at Ebury – Izzy and Elizabeth – for seeing this book's potential, and for bringing it to life with so much care. In doing so, you've made a dream come true.

Thank you to Liz and Max for the stunning photographs and cups of tea, and Sophie and Adam at Scramble London for cooking these recipes so incredibly beautifully.

Last but not least, thank you to my partner, Gordon, for your incomparable patience, support, love and constant laughter. You are the only person to have eaten almost every recipe in this book, and to have put up with a fridge, kitchen and living room filled with ingredients for weeks on end. Thank you for always believing in and celebrating me, even when I do too many things. I love you!

Oh, and to my perfect sausage dog, Barolo. I have no words other than I'm sorry I didn't let you eat more of the chicken.

Ebury Press

UK | USA | Canada | Ireland | Australia
India | New Zealand | South Africa

Ebury Press is part of the Penguin Random House group of companies whose addresses can be found at global.penguinrandomhouse.com

Penguin Random House UK
One Embassy Gardens, 8 Viaduct Gardens,
London SW11 7BW

penguin.co.uk
global.penguinrandomhouse.com

First published by Ebury Press in 2025
2

Copyright © Clem Haxby 2025
Photography © Haarala Hamilton 2025

Photography pages 6–7 © Rebecca Hope
Recipe page 104 credited to Darina Allen at Ballymalloe Cookery School
Recipes pages 124–6 credited to Christina Soteriou

The moral right of the author has been asserted.

Penguin Random House values and supports copyright. Copyright fuels creativity, encourages diverse voices, promotes freedom of expression and supports a vibrant culture. Thank you for purchasing an authorised edition of this book and for respecting intellectual property laws by not reproducing, scanning or distributing any part of it by any means without permission. You are supporting authors and enabling Penguin Random House to continue to publish books for everyone. No part of this book may be used or reproduced in any manner for the purpose of training artificial intelligence technologies or systems. In accordance with Article 4(3) of the DSM Directive 2019/790, Penguin Random House expressly reserves this work from the text and data mining exception.

Publishing Director: Elizabeth Bond
Assistant Editor: Izzy Frost
Production Controller: Percie Bridgwater
Designer: Emma Wells, Studio Nic+Lou
Photographer: Haarala Hamilton
Food Stylists: Scramble LDN
Food Styling Assistant: Romilly Dent
Prop Stylist: Charlie Phillips
Copyeditor: Jane Birch
Proofreader: Tara O'Sullivan
Indexer: Lisa Footitt

Colour origination by Altaimage Ltd
Printed and bound in Germany by Mohn Media GmbH

The authorised representative in the EEA is Penguin Random House Ireland, Morrison Chambers, 32 Nassau Street, Dublin D02 YH68.

A CIP catalogue record for this book is available from the British Library

ISBN 9781529949124

Penguin Random House is committed to a sustainable future for our business, our readers and our planet. This book is made from Forest Stewardship Council® certified paper.